What Parents Need to Know About Sibling Abuse

Breaking the Cycle of Violence

What Parents Need to Know About Sibling Abuse

Breaking the Cycle of Violence

by Vernon R. Wiehe, Ph.D.

BONNEVILLE BOOKS™
Springville, Utah

ISBN: 1-55517-586-4
v.1

Published by Bonneville Books
Imprint of Cedar Fort Inc.
www.cedarfort.com

Distributed by:

Typeset by Kristin Nelson
Cover design by Adam Ford
Cover design © 2002 by Lyle Mortimer

Printed in the United States of America
10 9 8 7 6 5 4 3 2 1

Printed on acid-free paper

Library of Congress Cataloging-in-Publication Data

Wiehe, Vernon R.
 What parents need to know about sibling abuse : breaking the cycle of
violence / by Vernon R. Wiehe.
   p. cm.
Includes bibliographical references.
 ISBN 1-55517-586-4
 1. Sibling abuse--Popular works. I. Title.
 RJ507.S53 W53 2002
 618.92'85822--dc21
                                    2001006243

iv

What Parents Need to Know About Sibling Abuse

Breaking the Cycle of Violence

I dedicate this book to my loving wife,
Donna.
This year marks our 40th wedding anniversary.

Acknowledgments

I wish to thank the many adults who participated in my research that forms the basis of this book. Their willingness to respond to my questions about the abuse they experienced as a child from a sibling will help parents cope with sibling rivalry that is out of control or prevent such abuse from occurring.

I want to express my deepest appreciation to Ann West who served as my editor in preparing the manuscript. She had the arduous task of turning a university professor's way of writing into a text that is easy to understand and a pleasure to read.

Finally, thanks to my wife for her support over the years of my research and writing.

Violence is wordlessness; it begins where human conversation breaks down.

A MacArthur Fellow

Chapter 1

Setting the Scene

"Husband in Rage Beats Wife in Parking Lot"

"Father Accused of Shaking Crying Baby
Causing Child's Death"

"Stepfather Found Guilty of Sexually Abusing Stepdaughter"

"Teenage Brother Shoots Younger Brother
After Heated Argument"

Headlines exposing violence in families appear repeatedly in our newspapers and on television. They appear so frequently that we have almost become immune to them. They have virtually lost their impact.

In a nation that is a world power—one of the richest, most educated, and most technologically advanced—what is this way we treat those with whom we live most closely, the members of our family? Violence in the American family is a tragedy. It is an affliction that plagues our nation, sparing not even our children.

Family violence was first brought to public attention in 1980 following the publication of a study titled, *Behind Closed Doors: Violence in the American Family.* This research, known as the *National Family Violence Survey,* involved 2,175 American families.[1] Up to that time, society had held the erroneous view

1

that whatever went on behind the closed doors of the family's home was no one else's business. Thus, husbands could strike their wives, parents could beat their children, siblings could attack each other, and adult children could neglect or abuse their elderly parents. The results of this research were shocking. The conclusion was that behind the closed doors of the family home, violence was rampant in American families.

The National Family Violence Survey was repeated ten years later, this time involving 6,002 families.[2] Again, the amount of violence occurring in American families was overwhelming.

One particularly shocking conclusion was reached in these two studies that forms the basis of this book. This conclusion is so important that it is paraphrased in bold type as follows:

Children are the most violent people of all in American families. Violence that occurs between or among children in a family—sibling violence— is the most prevalent form of family violence. An estimated 800 out of 1,000 children in a single year hit a brother or sister. More than half of them engage in what might be labeled "severe violence" in the form of kicking, punching, biting, choking, or attacks with a knife or gun. Two-thirds of American children ages 15 to 17 assault a sibling at least once during the course of a year. Over a third of these assaults have a high probability of causing injury to the victim. These incredible rates of sibling violence make the high rates of other forms of family violence, such as parents abusing children or spouses abusing each other, seem modest by comparison.[3]

What is being talked about here is a type of family violence that has largely been overlooked—sibling abuse, the physical and emotional harm of one sibling by another. Although society recognizes child, partner, and elder abuse as significant social problems with dire consequences for individuals and families, the same cannot yet be said for sibling abuse.[4]

This is due to several reasons: 1) Social movements first developed around child, partner, and elder abuse. For example, various advocacy groups have brought to public attention this type of abuse, resulting in the passage of legislation and the formation of social agencies with the purpose of detection, treatment, and prevention. However, the same has not occurred for sibling abuse. 2) Hitting, pushing, slapping and name-calling are so common among siblings that these behaviors for the most part are not regarded as violence. On the basis of their own experiences as children, many parents consider physical and emotional sibling abuse as simply "sibling rivalry" and a normal part of growing up. Some parents even incorrectly assume that such behavior is good preparation for managing what one has to face later as an adult in interactions with others.

Let's go back to the conclusions (in bold type) reached by the two national studies of family violence—siblings are the most violent individuals in American families. The way siblings treat each other physically and emotionally is by far worse than the way parents abuse their children or the way adults treat their intimate partners. That is, many siblings are abusive, harmful, and destructive to each other. Is this normal behavior? Is this just a passing phase that siblings go through? Hardly!

The premise of this book is that the violence which siblings display toward each other is the beginning of a pattern of violence that often continues throughout life. For example, physical and emotional abuse of one sibling by another can easily be seen also in the way these children relate to their peers. Violence in peer relationships is called "bullying." And, if siblings relate to each other and to their peers with violence, what is going to keep them from relating in a similar fashion to the other sex when they begin dating? This is known as "dating violence." If the dating relationship is tainted by violence, the assumption can be made that when the violent sibling moves in (cohabits) with a girlfriend or later marries, this relationship also will be strewn with violence. This is known as "partner abuse." When the violent sibling has children, violence can be expected to appear in that relationship, known as "child abuse."

Do you see how the pattern of violence begets violence? This cycle gets repeated over and over in different and various relationships. Like a hurricane, it viciously sucks up victims in a whirlwind of destruction. Beginning in the home, violence forms a pattern between siblings, then spirals outward to other relationships.

The finger of blame is not pointed at all siblings. They had to learn how to be violent from somewhere. Where did they learn such behavior? The two national studies on family violence and other research present an answer to that question:

> Those siblings who are most violent to each other live in homes in which the parents are abusive to each other and in which the children are disciplined by spanking or corporal punishment. Also, children learn violence from watching TV and videos and from playing violent video games.

This book examines sibling violence as the insidious breeding ground or hotbed for later violence in life. In early Spring, we can assist nature by planting seeds or young starts in the protective climate of a warm hotbed. A hotbed is the place where roses or weeds will get a hardy head start. We hope to germinate only the finest plants that will later grace our flowerbeds and gardens. Just the same, both harmony and violence are rooted in the family climate. When violence between siblings is established in this hotbed, it naturally makes way for other types of interpersonal violence—bullying, dating violence, and child, partner, and elder abuse.

Since the two *National Family Violence Surveys*, progress has been made in recognizing, treating, and preventing family violence. However, family violence continues and children are learning how to pass on violent ways to the next generation. Or, they become so hurt that they live in a world of suspicion, fear, and misery. Something needs to be done to stop this cycle that begins with siblings.

How can parents recognize sibling abuse? What can parents do to stop sibling abuse in their families? How can the cycle of violence be interrupted? These are some of the questions that the following chapters answer.

Format of the Book

The first chapter explores sibling abuse in the context of family violence—its various types and forms and how to think about violence. Critical to the understanding of sibling abuse and family violence in general are several theories of aggression taken from social psychology. Subsequent chapters discuss details of physical, emotional, and sexual abuse inflicted by one sibling on another. These chapters focus on how to recognize abuse, why each type of abuse occurs, the way such violence affects survivors, recommendations and resources for parents and educators; and, ways sibling abuse can be interrupted or prevented. Research identifies two factors as important to understanding why siblings are abusive: First, the abuse may be occurring between the parents and second, the parents may be using corporal punishment on their children. The final chapters are devoted to these subjects.

May this book give you a better understanding of sibling abuse within families as a major social challenge in American society. If you are a survivor of abuse from a sibling or are experiencing violence in your family, especially among children, the book may encourage you to seek professional help. For others, after reading this book you may wish to work or volunteer in one of the many social service agencies in your community dedicated to assisting survivors and preventing a new generation of victims of violence.

Something to Think About

Why do you think families are violent?

Have you observed in your children or personally experienced any of the types of violence identified in the *cycle of violence*?

1 Straus, M., Gelles, R., & Steinmetz, S. (1980). *Behind closed doors: Violence in the American family.* Garden City, NY: Anchor.

2 Straus, M., & Gelles, R. (1990). *Physical violence in American families: Risk factors and adaptations to violence in 8,145 families.* New Brunswick, NJ: Transaction Publishers.

3 Straus, M., & Gelles, R. (1988). How violent are American families? Estimates from the National Family Violence Resurvey and other studies. In G. Hotaling, D. Finkelhor, J. Kirkpatrick, and M. Strauss (Eds.), *Family abuse and its consequences: New directions in research* (pp. 14-36). Newbury Park, CA: Sage.

4 The term *partner* rather than *spouse* abuse is used because research shows that abuse is one and a half to two times greater among cohabiting couples than among married couples. See, for example, Ellis, D., & Dekeseredy, W. (1989). Marital status and woman abuse: The DAD model. *International Journal of Sociology of the Family, 19,* 67-87.

Our home was a three ring circus of violence. Dad was abusing my mother; my parents were abusing us children, and my brother was abusing me.

A sibling abuse survivor

Chapter 2

At Home With Violence;
Waking Up to an American Tragedy

Before we look at sibling abuse, it is important to understand the larger picture of families and the violence that takes place within them. The following terms relate to the types and forms of family violence.

What Is Family Violence?

There are four types of family violence—child, sibling, partner, and elder abuse. Bullying and dating violence, which are actually forms of interpersonal violence rather than family violence, are included in our discussion of family violence because they are part of the cycle of violence. Violence appears in three forms in each of these types—physical, emotional, and sexual abuse.

Child abuse, as the term implies, is the physical, emotional, or sexual abuse of a child by a parent, step-parent, relative, or parent surrogate. *Partner abuse,* also referred to as *domestic violence,* generally is defined as the abuse of a woman by her husband or by a male companion with whom she is living. The term *spouse* is avoided because many couples are not married, but

7

simply living together. Domestic violence can also occur when a male is assaulted by his female partner or between two individuals of the same sex who are living together as a couple. *Elder abuse* describes the abuse of an elderly person by an adult child, a relative, or a caregiver. *Sibling abuse*, often inappropriately excused as sibling rivalry, the main focus of this book, typically occurs in a family context between or among brothers and sisters. *Bullying* occurs among peers and often is seen in a school setting. It consists primarily of physical and emotional abuse, although it can have sexual overtones. *Dating violence*, as the term implies, is physical, emotional, or sexual abuse in the context of the dating relationship.

Now consider the different forms of family violence. *Physical abuse* generally involves willful acts of violence of one family member against another. For example, individuals might hit, bite, kick, or slap and use objects such as a belt, stick, rod, or bat. However, violent actions by a parent or family member sometimes lead to injury, harm, or even death despite the absence of a willful intent. Perhaps a parent whips a child as a form of punishment and the intent is not to harm the child but welts or bruises occur as a result. Or, an older brother wants to "teach his younger brother a lesson" for borrowing his ball glove without asking for permission. The older brother jumps on the back of his younger sibling. The younger is thrown to the floor causing damage to his spine. Even so, this behavior is regarded as abusive because the consequences have resulted in an injury.

Emotional abuse or psychological maltreatment is defined as destructive verbal behavior in which one family member attacks another's self-esteem and social competence. For instance, an older sibling may intend to ridicule, insult, threaten, or belittle a younger one. Many people are unaware not only of the serious damage that emotional abuse does to a child but even what constitutes emotional abuse. Figure 2.1 identifies various ways in which emotional abuse of a child occurs by an adult. Note that a perpetrator who engages in emotional abuse may be someone of any age, gender, or relationship to the child. Emotional abuse is difficult to document because of the absence of physical evidence; therefore, incidents of emotional abuse seldom reach the court. Although emotional abuse can occur alone, researchers identify this behavior as a core component and major destructive force accompanying physical and sexual abuse.

Figure 2.1

Types of Emotional Abuse

Rejecting. Treating a child different from siblings or peers in ways suggesting a dislike for the child; actively refusing to act to help or acknowledge a child's request for help.

Degrading. Calling a child "stupid" or similar names; labeling as inferior, publicly humiliating a child.

Terrorizing. Threatening to physically hurt or forcing a child to observe violence directed toward loved ones; leaving a young child unattended.

Isolating. Locking a child in a closet or in a room alone for an extended period of time; refusing to allow interactions or relationships with peers or adults outside the family.

Corrupting. Teaching or reinforcing behavior that degrades children who are racially or ethnically different; teaching or reinforcing criminal behavior; providing antisocial and inappropriate models as normal, usual, or appropriate.

Exploiting. Keeping a child at home in the role of a servant or surrogate parent in lieu of school attendance; encouraging a child to participate in illegal or dysfunctional behavior.

Denying Emotional Responsiveness. Ignoring a child's attempts to interact; mechanistic child handling devoid of hugs, stroking, kisses, and talk.[1]

Sexual abuse is defined as the use of another person for sexual gratification without the latter's consent. In some instances, such as for young children, the victims are not able to consent. Contact forms of sexual abuse include, for example, inappropriately touching a child or requesting a child to sexually touch an older sibling or adult. Non-contact sexual abuse includes indecent exposure to a child or forcing a child to observe sexual behavior. Sexual abuse in the context of partner abuse is referred to as *marital rape*. In the context of a dating relationship, it is known as *date rape.*

Other terms used in this book are *perpetrator, victim,* and *survivor.* The individual engaging in the abusive behavior is referred to as the perpetrator. The person who is the object or target of the abuse, especially at the time it is occurring, is the victim. Individuals who have been victims of abuse generally prefer to call themselves survivors. Being a victim implies helplessness. Being a survivor, on the other hand, implies strength, persistence and healing, despite the abuse that has occurred.

Is Family Violence on the Rise?

Statistical data show that the various types of family violence have increased dramatically over the past decades; nevertheless, these data need to be put into perspective:

First, until as recently as 1980, when the book *Behind Closed Doors: Violence in the American Family* was published, we had no idea of how pervasive family violence was in American society. This does not mean that abuse did not exist before that time; rather, we now generally regard as abusive or violent certain behavior in families that previously was overlooked.

Second, little statistical data on the different types of family violence were gathered prior to the early 1980's. Moreover, when incidences of family violence began to be recorded in subsequent years, statistical data were gathered by different agencies using different definitions. For example, data on child abuse used varying definitions and were recorded by several national organizations including the National Center on Child Abuse Prevention Research, the American Association for Protecting Children (AAPC), and the National Committee to Prevent Child Abuse (NCPCA). You will notice in Figure 2:2 that the number of reported cases for child abuse in 1998 decreased slightly from the previous year but rose again in 1999, the latest year on which statistical data are currently available. This does not necessarily mean that child abuse incidents have gone down, but more likely that there have been changes in data collection methods for several states.

Third, a sharp increase in the number of cases reported over the past several decades may be due in part to legislation that provides anonymity to individuals seeing and reporting such incidents, thereby protecting them from possible legal action. Also, increases in reporting might be because society has become more aware over the years about different types of family violence as movies, television, and even popular literature incorporate these topics.

Fourth, technical sophistication of data gathering, storage, and retrieval has made it possible for state social service agencies across the country to quickly collect data from even remote areas of the state and relay this to national reporting organizations. Thus, the number of incidents of abuse being seen in their offices can be reported rapidly and frequently with seemingly little effort. Prior to the availability of this technology, statistical data gathering was a tedious, cumbersome and less reliable process.

In any case, no one would deny that we live in a very violent society. Today, the use of drugs, the availability of guns, and the frequency of violent acts portrayed in the media make it apparent that violence, not only in the form of assaults and murders among strangers but also occurring in the setting of the family, is more prevalent now than at the turn of the century.

A few statistics will give a clearer picture of the extent of family violence in American society. Remember that whenever statistics on family violence are cited, they represent only the "tip of the iceberg." That is, many such incidents are never reported to police or to social service agencies. Also, some violent behavior may not be recognized as abuse, as is the case with sibling abuse that is regarded as merely sibling rivalry.

The American Humane Association collected data on child abuse from states from 1976 to 1987. In subsequent years, these statistics were compiled by the National Center on Child Abuse Prevention Research, currently a program of Prevent Child Abuse America. Figure 2:2 shows the number of reported cases of child abuse and the estimated number of children per 1,000 population who were victims of child abuse. (These figures also include reports of child abuse neglect.) Child neglect is defined as parental failure to provide children with adequate food, shelter, medical care and general physical care. In 1999, the latest year for which data are available, over 3 million children were reported as victims, a rate of 46 per 1,000 children in our country.

Figure 2:2

National Estimates of Child Abuse and Neglect Reports, 1976– 1998

Year	Estimated Number of Children Reported	Estimated Number of Children per 1,000 Population
1976	669,000	10.1
1977	838,000	12.8
1978	836,000	12.9
1979	988,000	15.4
1980	1,154,000	18.1
1981	1,225,000	19.4
1982	1,262,000	20.1
1983	1,477,000	23.6
1984	1,727,000	27.3
1985	1,928,000	30.6
1986	2,086,000	32.8
1987	2,157,000	34.0
1988	2,265,000	35.0
1989	2,435,000	38.0
1990	2,557,000	40.0
1991	2,684,000	42.0
1992	2,909,000	45.0
1993	2,967,000	45.0
1994	3,062,000	45.0
1995	3,105,000	45.0
1996	3,120,000	45.0
1997	3,232,000	46.0
1998	3,193,000	46.0
1999	3,244,000	46.0

Many cases of child abuse, sexual abuse in particular, are never reported. Often victims blame themselves for the abuse and, therefore, remain silent. Or, if the perpetrator is a family member or well-known to the family, the family may be reluctant to press charges. However, a national study gives us a picture of the extent to which sexual abuse occurs.[2] A sample of 2,626 adult men and women nationwide were surveyed by telephone to determine if they had experienced any such abuse as a child, age eighteen and under. Thirty-eight percent of the women and sixteen percent of the men recalled a history of sexual abuse. The median age for sexual abuse was approximately nine years old. One-half of the perpetrators were authority figures in the children's lives.

Regarding partner abuse, the National Coalition Against Domestic Violence estimates that at least four million incidents of domestic violence are reported against women every year.[3] In the United States, a woman is more likely to be assaulted, injured, raped, or killed by a male partner than by any other type of assailant.

For several reasons, incidents of elder abuse, even more so than other types of family violence, are often not reported. The victims may be dependent upon adult children who are abusing them and thereby cannot risk reporting what is occurring. Also, elderly individuals with Alzheimer's are at greatest risk for abuse but may not be able to access resources where they can receive assistance or report the abuse they are experiencing. Prevalence studies on elder abuse suggest that this problem occurs at the rate of approximately thirty two per one thousand population, with physical abuse being the most prevalent form of abuse. Nearly sixty percent of the perpetrators are spouses, with the remainder being children (adult sons and daughters), grandchildren, siblings, and boarders.[4]

Incidents of sibling abuse are seldom reported to authorities, thus prevalence rates for this type of abuse are not available. As research has shown, eight hundred out of a one thousand children ages three to seventeen hit a brother or sister during a single year and more than half engage in what researchers label as "severe violence," such as kicking, punching, biting, choking, or attacks with a knife or gun. For children ages fifteen to seventeen, the data showed that two-thirds of American children assault a sibling at least once during the course of a year, and in over a third of these cases, the assault involves an act with a relatively high probability of causing injury.[5]

Incidents of bullying rarely are reported to authorities, thus prevalence rates are not available for this type of interpersonal violence. However, the National Association of School Psychologists estimate that 160,000 children miss school in a single day for fear of being bullied. Regarding dating violence, research indicates that more than one in ten teens experience physical violence in their dating relationships.[6] Again, these figures represent only the tip of the iceberg, because out of embarrassment and fear, most teens never report incidents of dating violence.

Why So Much Violence?

Why do family members physically, emotionally, or even sexually abuse other family members? How can we understand such violence? Theories, developed through research methods, help us answer these questions.

The purpose of a theory might be compared to the function of a magnifying glass. Imagine that you have a piece of paper in front of you with such very small print that, when you attempt to read the words, the message is a blur of ink. But, when you look at the small print through a magnifying glass, the ink blob begins to take the shape of letters. Soon, the combinations of letters form words, and the words come together in sentences to present a message you can read and understand.

Theory acts in a similar fashion to explain the complexities of human behavior. For example: an older brother observes that his younger sister is developing breasts as she enters puberty. He makes comments about her breasts in a derogatory manner and has teasingly touched her breasts in the absence of her parents. Her parents ignore the brother's comments although they are embarrassing to his younger sister. Earlier, the father had told an off-color joke at the dinner table, the punch line having focused on a blonde with large breasts.

When reading about an incident such as this, we cannot fully comprehend why a brother would emotionally and sexually abuse his sister by making comments about her developing breasts and by touching them. We may perceive the abuse as we would static on a radio or snow on a television screen. We call this response to information *dissonance* because it just doesn't make sense. Presented with what we don't understand, we often resort to myths or stereotypical ways of thinking about the situation. Unfortunately, this may cause us to incorrectly perceive the problem or even to place the blame on the victim. However, using theory or what research has learned allows us to understand with a broader perspective. Regarding the example above, social learning theory or the concept of *modeling* (a theory you will be introduced to in the next chapter), helps us understand the brother's abusive behavior. The boy has learned this behavior, at least in part, from his father and is modeling his father's behavior which was reflected in the joke he told his family that made fun of a blonde and her breasts. This is not to say other factors are not also important, for example, parents' not interrupting abuse when they see it, modeling behavior of peers and what is seen on TV, and psychological problems of a child.

We can also think of theory as a framework for examining human behavior. In the physical sciences, in medicine for example, particular bacteria are said to *cause* a particular illness. The physician then prescribes an antibody that will destroy the cause or the bacteria. We cannot apply this method in the social sciences. Rather than trying to identify a single cause of sibling abuse, we prefer to talk about *related* or *associated factors*. Therefore, we use models that are *multi-causal*. This is where theory enters the picture. Research, or the use of empirical methodology, enables us to identify these various factors and form sets of conditions under which certain acts are expected to take place.

Some people attempt to point to a single causal factor of what ails society, such as the abuse of drugs or alcohol. Although it may be possible in physical sciences like medicine to identify a single bacteria that causes a certain illness, this is not true for the social sciences. It is just not that simple. For example, research may suggest a relationship between substance abuse and partner abuse, but many people abuse drugs or alcohol yet do not abuse their partner. There is no single cause for problems-in-living, no *social bacteria,* as it were.

Two different levels of theory better help understand sibling abuse in the context of family violence. In the next chapter, several general theories of aggression from social psychology give us an idea why human beings are violent toward each other. In the following chapters, however, we will examine more specific theoretical factors identified from research related to sibling abuse in the context of family violence.

The next time you read about an incident of family violence that you find revolting or disgusting, remember the magnifying glass. Even though your sense of decency and respect for others may cause you to say, "How could someone do this?" Stop!—think before you lash out in anger against the perpetrator. Now, view the same incident from a theoretical perspective. Begin to truly understand the incident. Do not confuse understanding the problem with condoning or approving of the behavior—just like researchers and educators do, attempt to understand the abuse and what factors are associated with each circumstance. This way of thinking also assists educators and service providers in dealing with perpetrators and survivors. When research identifies the factors related, then methods of intervention, treatment, and prevention can be more effectively planned and implemented.

Something to Think About

The statement was made that we live in a violent society. Of what kind of violence are you aware? Do you think families are more violent today than in the past?

The next time you read the newspaper, identify the news items that relate to violence. Are any of these stories reporting the types and forms of violence identified in this chapter?

1 Hart, S., Germain, R., & Brassard, M. (1987). The challenge: To better understand and combat the psychological maltreatment of children and youth. In M. Brassard, R. Germain, & S. Hart (Eds.), *Psychological maltreatment of children and youth* (pp. 3-24). New York: Pergamon.

2 Finkelhor, D., Hotaling, G., Lewis, I., & Smith, C. (1990). Sexual abuse in a national survey of adult men and women: Prevalence, characteristics, and risk factors. *Child Abuse & Neglect, 14*, 14-28.

3 National Coalition Against Domestic Violence. Membership and other information available from the coalition at P.O. Box 18749, Denver, CO. 80218-0749. Telephone: (303) 839-1852.

4 Pillemer, K., & Finkelhor, D. (1988). The prevalence of elder abuse: A random sample survey. *The Gerontologist, 28*, 71-57.

5 Straus, M., & Gelles, R. (1988). How violent are American families? Estimates from the National Family Violence Resurvey and other studies. In G. Hotaling, D. Finkelhor, J. Kirkpatrick, & M. Strauss (Eds.), *Family abuse and its consequences: New directions in research* (pp. 14-36). Newbury Park, CA: Sage.

6 http://www.brown.edu/Student Services/SAPE/dv-stats.htm

Our behavior toward each other is the strangest, most unpredictable, and most unaccountable of all the phenomena with which we are obliged to live. In all of nature there is nothing so threatening to humanity as humanity itself.

Lewis Thomas

Chapter 3

Why Do We Hurt Each Other?

Why do people behave aggressively toward each other, especially family members? How can we understand such behavior? Before we examine four foundational theories, another question should be considered: What is *aggression*? Aggression is generally defined as injurious or destructive behavior of one person directed toward another. Most important, the person who is the target of this behavior does not want to be treated in that way. The term *behavior* refers to physical and verbal acts. Physical acts of aggression in family violence may include hitting, slapping, pushing, or even the use of a weapon. Verbal aggression occurs in the form of insulting, demeaning, or hurtful comments.

Behavior that is aggressive should be distinguished from behavior that is assertive, even though these two terms are often used interchangeably. Someone says, for example, "He's an aggressive salesman," to denote a successful marketing approach. However, a company's sales strategy to customers does not represent behavior that intends to be injurious or destructive, that harms, hurts, or destroys another person. Thus, a more appropriate word to describe this behavior is *assertive*.

To be assertive implies stating one's position forcefully, boldly, and with conviction, to be persistent and persuasive. Being assertive also includes standing up for one's rights in interpersonal relationships, which is a skill that can be learned. For example, children must be assertive, not aggressive, in standing up to a sibling who is sexually abusing them.

Is There a Biological Basis for Aggression?

Freud proposed that aggression was an inborn instinct or drive, a self-generating force rather than a reaction or response to a situation as thought by later theorists.[1] Freud felt that all human beings have two basic drives: aggressive and sexual. The aggressive drive was seen as destructive—the death instinct. Destructive energy could be directed toward others or turned in on oneself in self-punishing behavior or even suicide. The aggressive drive could also be diverted into positive channels, such as in the pursuit of a career or a hobby.

Freud theorized that aggressive and sexual energy, similar to steam under pressure, must be released periodically. Therefore, instinctual energies within the human psyche may need occasional expression. Release might occur directly in the display of aggressive behavior or indirectly—through work, a hobby, competitive games, and sports.

Later theorists studying animal behavior also accepted Freud's view of aggression. Aggression was necessary for the survival of a species,[2] according to Darwin's principle that only the fittest will survive. However, animals generally do not display aggression against their own species, except for dominance, territory, or mates in order that the species can continue to exist. These theorists suggested that humans did not evolve such a protective inhibition against aggression toward their own kind. With the invention of weapons and with no brake against directing aggression toward other humans, our species is placed in a position of potential self-destruction. Thus, we must find ways to drain off or sublimate this aggressive energy or instinct. The views of these theorists have been subjected to extensive criticism, but the fact remains that human beings are capable of hurting each other.

Social psychologists, on the other hand, disagree with the instinctual theory because it is based on circular reasoning. It provides no empirical evidence to support the idea of aggression as an instinct or drive. For example, the question "Why do birds flock together?" may prompt someone to answer that birds have an instinct to flock together. If confronted for evidence to support this behavior, someone may reply, "Just look at birds, they are flocking together."[3] This explanation gives no additional concrete information about the cause of the behavior and is not considered "evidence."

The instinctual theory of aggression is also criticized on the basis that if this were a universal trait in all human beings, then everyone would display aggression. Anthropologists, however, have studied cultures whose members do not display aggressive behavior, such as the Philippine Tasady tribe who have no word for war.[4] Also, the Iroquois Indians were known to be very peaceful, responding in self-defense only after being attacked by European settlers.[5]

This is not to deny a relationship between aggression and biological influences. Complex neural systems in the brain when stimulated electrically or chemically can promote aggressive behavior. Similar effects appear after certain types of head injuries, and victims sometimes react with rage unlike ordinary anger.[6] Their rage may be sudden and unpredictable, like a storm of overwhelming fury triggered by some trivial stimulus.

Biochemical changes, especially in the brain, are also a factor in aggression. For example, alcohol and drugs may lower restraints against aggression.[7] We have all heard of "fighting drunks" and "funny drunks." Hence, substance abuse is a signif-icant factor in the various types of abuse comprising family violence. In addition, children prenatally exposed to drugs are thought to be later at risk to engage in violent behaviors. Studies also show the dysfunction of substance-abusing parents produces an unsuitable, inconsistent environment for children expected to learn appropriate pro-social behaviors.[8]

Residues from lead-based paints also can act as a brain poison interfering with a person's ability to keep aggression in check. A recent study found that boys from an inner city neighborhood with above-normal lead values in their bones were more likely to engage in aggressive and delinquent behaviors than a similar group carrying less lead.[9]

Genetic factors effect aggressiveness as well. Differences in temperament can be observed shortly after birth, even among siblings. Anyone with more than one child in his family can relate to how unique in temperament each child can be. These traits observed early in life may endure into adulthood.[10]

Psychobiologists and evolutionary psychologists are currently studying the biological basis for violence. Research has documented a relationship between levels of the neurotransmitter serotonin and impaired impulse control, violent outbursts, and increased aggressiveness.[11] This study in humans has been preceded by research on serotonin levels in vervet monkeys. It was found that monkeys with the highest ranking in their clan have the highest serotonin levels and those with a low ranking have the lowest levels and are most violent. The influence of environment, however, is not ruled out. The social environment, for example, living in a ghetto neighborhood where crime and poverty prevail may biologically shape individuals.

In summary, although there is little empirical support for the theory of aggression being a biological drive, as suggested by Freud, there still is a biological basis for aggression. This can be seen in genetic differences relative to aggression and in the effect on the brain of head injuries, lead poisoning, and the use of drugs and alcohol.

When Is Frustration Like a Time-Bomb?

First proposed in the late 1930s, this theory suggests that aggression stems from frustration when a person experiences blockage or interference in attaining a goal.[12] The greater the motivation is to achieve the goal, the greater the frustration. Frustration builds up until it is released—usually back on its source or on another object or person. For example, a younger brother might be frustrated that he does not achieve academically in school like his older sister. His teachers add to the frustration by recalling when they had his sister in class and what a fine student she was. The younger brother takes out his frustration on his sister by being physically abusive toward her, especially whenever grades in school are mentioned.

Some types of frustration seem more volatile than others. If people believe the circumstances are unintended, caused by what is beyond anyone's control, accidental, or justified, they will be less likely to respond with aggression.[13] For instance, Tom and Mark are twin sixteen-year-old brothers. Tom is planning on meeting Mark for a movie after he finishes his part-time job. Tom waits outside the theater, but Mark does not appear. He is frustrated over what is happening. Sirens are heard, and a short time later, Tom hears someone saying that an accident on the freeway has blocked traffic. Tom begins to understand why his brother has not appeared at the theater. Apparently, Mark is caught in a traffic jam; his absence is not intentional. Tom's frustration begins to dissipate.

The same scenario may be repeated under different circumstances. This time there is no traffic accident. When Tom returns home, he confronts Mark about not showing up at the movie theater. Mark responds by saying that he decided that he didn't want to see the movie because someone had told him it wasn't any good. Tom's frustration of waiting for his brother coupled with his brother's intention of not showing up and letting Tom wait provokes an angry response in Tom. Tom's anger is evident in the conversation he has with Mark and by his resolve to never again go anywhere with his brother. Thus, the understanding of one's circumstances is a key to how that person will respond to frustration.

For researchers to study the frustration-aggression connection, a group of children was shown but not allowed to enter a room full of toys. Only after a period of time could they enter the room and play. A similar group was given immediate access to the toys without having to wait. Those children who did not get to play right away demonstrated aggressive behavior when they finally got to the toys. They smashed them and in general were very destructive, whereas the children who were allowed immediate access to their goal did not display such behavior.[14] That is, aggression was evident only in the second group experiencing no frustration.

Frustration at the societal level also can stimulate aggressive behavior. The media presents to young people many desirable products—stereos, television sets, computers, cell phones. The impression is given that everyone should have these items. An adolescent living with his single mother in a poverty ghetto who cannot find a job and is doing poorly in school, in part because he must attend an inferior school in his neighborhood, becomes frustrated that he cannot reach the goal of purchasing these items. He acts out his frustration with several neighborhood youth by holding up a shopkeeper and stealing a stereo and computer.

Parents who are under stress due to physical, emotional, and financial problems, factors that may be regarded as frustrating, are at risk for engaging in physical and emotional child abuse. The same can occur in partner/spouse relationships. For example, a prolonged labor strike or the inability to find employment can create stress for a parent due to the inability to adequately provide for the family. These incidents of abuse may not be reflected in statistical data because often they are not reported, however, the incidents generally come out later in counseling or therapy when a family seeks help for its problems.

Social psychologists have conducted numerous laboratory experiments to test the frustration-aggression theory. One finding is that two prerequisites may be necessary for frustration to trigger aggression: both a readiness to act aggressively and the presence of external cues.[15] Even after frustration that could easily result in an aggressive response, there must be a readiness to act in this manner. A sibling might be very frustrated by what his brother or sister does to him, but this doesn't mean that the frustration will necessarily result in aggressive behavior. Also, external aversive stimuli, rather than frustration alone, are needed to set off such behavior. For example, if another sibling joins in making fun of a child, this may further provoke him to act in anger. Aversive factors—such as physiological arousal, verbal and physical attack, uncomfortable temperatures—especially heat, and the use of drugs and alcohol, stimulate a "state of arousal."

External conditions also can affect the relationship between frustration and aggression, known as "the weapons effect."[16] Researchers found that the presence or availability of weapons can prompt or "prime" individuals to act aggressively. Hence, the availability of guns in American society may be a significant factor contributing to family violence.

Approximately 200 million guns are in private hands in the United States. A recent study of guns and schools revealed that nearly one million students carried a gun to school during a single school year. Nearly one-half of these students were armed with a gun six or more times during the same period of time.[17] The impact from the availability of guns can be seen in comparison figures for the United States and other countries relative to the number of people who are murdered with the use of a gun. In one recent year, "handguns were used to murder 13 people in

Australia; 33 people in Great Britain; sixty people in Japan; 128 in Canada; and more than 13,000 in the United States."[18] The leading cause of death among teenagers is from gunshot wounds. Nationwide, fifteen teens are killed by guns each day—some by accident.[19] The Columbine shootings, as well as shootings in other schools, provide an example of the availability of guns in our society and the horribly destructive outcome. Who would have thought fifteen years ago that children must enter their school by going through metal detectors.

Figure 3:1

Violence and Guns

Pat Oliphant
UNIVERSAL PRESS

The availability of guns as well as the role guns play in violence has prompted several major Protestant, Roman Catholic, and Jewish organizations to favor restrictions on handguns and assault weapons. The policy-making body of the

Presbyterian Church (U.S.A.) in its recent annual General Assembly passed a resolution calling on the denomination's 2.6 million members to begin removing handguns and assault weapons from their homes.

Is Aggression a Learned Behavior?

Aggressive behavior may be learned from observing others acting aggressively. This is known as *social learning theory*, based on the process of modeling—or in colloquial terms, "monkey see, monkey do." The imitation process was initially demonstrated in a study involving three- to five-year-olds, some of whom observed an adult behaving aggressively toward a large plastic "Bobo" doll and later imitated that behavior in their own play with the doll. By contrast, the youngsters in the study who had not observed the adult's aggressive behavior did not behave aggressively toward the doll when they played with it.[20]

It is critical for parents to be aware of how they act both toward each other and toward their children. The two National Family Violence Studies, referred to in the first chapter, found that the highest rates of sibling violence were associated with violence that was occurring between the parents. The children were "modeling" in their relationships to each other what they were observing in their parents. Or, conversely, the parents were demonstrating to their children how they should get along with each other—by being physically and emotionally abusive to their siblings.

Spanking in the form of hitting or slapping a child is another example of the way in which parents model aggressive behavior. Spanking suggests to children that aggression is an acceptable form of problem solving. Children punished in this manner have been shown to behave in the same way toward siblings and peers.[21] Many countries have passed legislation that prohibits parents from using corporal punishment with their children.

Figure 3.2
Countries Banning Corporal Punishment in Homes and Schools

Austria	Finland
Croatia	Italy
Cyprus	Latvia
Denmark	Norway
Sweden	

Source: http://www.religioustolerance.org/spanking.htm

Research also indicates that role models who are rewarded for their aggressive behavior are more likely to be imitated. When a behavior is rewarded, an individual is more likely to repeat that behavior; or the opposite, when a behavior is punished, the person is more likely to avoid the behavior. Also, people tend to imitate or model the behavior of others they regard as important, powerful, or successful.[22] These factors may in part explain the powerful effect that television and movie personalities have on viewers. Imagine the repercussion that fighting and killing scenes or aggressive behavior in sports has on children—especially when their idols are rewarded rather than punished.

The National Institute of Mental Health has reviewed extensive research on the relationship between television and aggressive behavior. Researchers at the Institute have concluded, on the basis of laboratory experiments and field studies, that violence on television does lead to aggressive behavior by children and teenagers who watch such programs.

The effects of violence can be passed on in several ways: 1) constant and repeated exposure to violence in the media may instigate or trigger aggressive behavior, depending upon the strength of the cue and the readiness of the observer; 2) repeated exposure in media programming may break down inhibitions against violence, thereby making the viewer more ready to engage in aggression modeled after what was seen; and 3) long-term exposure to violence in the media may have a desensitizing effect in that the violence may alter a viewer's sense of reality and give the viewer the impression that violence is a method of problem solving. The viewer may end up no longer reacting with revulsion to the violence or perceiving this as behavior to be avoided. For example, characters on television are shot to death but no one witnesses a funeral, grieving family or friends, or the struggles of a family to continue in life. More than likely, the character who was shot will appear soon in another role. The impact of the violence is lost on the viewer.

Listening to rap music in which the lyrics degrade women or portray them as wanting forced sex may promote sexually aggressive behavior. "Hoochie Mama," from 2 Live Crew's *Friday Soundtrack*, is a popular example (see Figure 3:3).

Figure 3.3

Text of the Rap Song, "Hoochie Mama"

Big booty hoes hop wit it!
Hoochie mamas hop wit it!
Let me see ya touch the ground.

I don't know ya reputation
but all the niggas in the hood say it's all good
but the bitch ain't shit, so ya need to make a switch
Smackin on ya lips with your hands on your hips

Trife and slimy, don't try me
Playin on the phone, you supposed to be grown
Bitch stop lyin, I ain't wit it
Keep runnin ya mouth and I'm a stick my dick in it
Hoochie Hoodrat needs ho trainin
Ghetto ass always complainin
Tryin to clown in front of my friends
By the way bitch, can I get those ends?
Fuck the asterisk you ain't no actress
Lay low the mattress, let a nigga scrag it
The bitch is full of dram
Hoochie hoodrat is a ho like a mom

Ho I love ya big brown eyes
and the way you shake your thighs
Acting like your so damn cute
Let a real nigga just knock them boots
I don't need no confrontation
All I want is an ejaculation
Cos I like them ghetto hoochies
One-two-light, pop that cochie
(Hoo wee!) Mommy style
Makin niggas smile, bitch get wild
Cos freaky shit is what I like
and I love to see two bitches dyke
My favorite job is 69
Bitch you know it's coochie time
Fuck what you heard and save ya drama
All I want is my hoochie mama.

Mama just don't understand
why I love your hoochie ass
Sex is what I need you for

I gotta good girl but I need a whore
I like my bitch promiscuous
Hot in the ass and ready to fuck
Foreplay your way, all way my way
Trick a freak and I hit it on Friday
Girl you know ya look so cute
Ridin round town in ya Daisy Duke
Come on over for a visit
Let a nigga ride in ya Civic
Cos I like them ghetto hoochies
One who got them big ol' booties
Save the drama for your mama
All I want is my hoochie mama

Chorus:
You ain't nothin but a hoochie mama
Hoodrat hoodrat hoochie mama!
She ain't nothin but a hoochie mama
Hoodrat hoodrat hoochie mama!

Source: http://www.ohhla.com/an...m_bside/hoochie.21c.txt

When watching videos and movies, the viewer visually is emotionally brought into the violence occurring on the screen. A particular concern which educators and health professionals have with videos that contain violent scenes is that children view the violent scenes devoid of the overall story. Violent scenes may be viewed over and over by children and even freeze-framed on the television. The result is that the violence is seen out of context, especially missing the consequences of the violence for the participants. The availability of videos in the home, either rented or owned, has added another dimension to the effects of violence on the family.[23] However, even print media showing graphic accounts of violence can produce a modeling effect. For example, national suicide levels increased following newspaper accounts of suicides.[24] Likewise, a significant rise in the number of homicides was found to occur several days after heavyweight fights.[25]

The modeling of self-destructive aggressive behavior was a factor in the death of several young people who copied a young man in the movie *The Program*. The movie character, a college football hero, following a dare from peers to prove that he had nerves of steel, laid down in the middle of a busy highway as cars and trucks sped past in the dark. Unlike the movie hero who survived, several adolescents were killed instantly when they modeled the stunt and were struck by traffic.

Some computer games may instigate aggressive behavior in players, as reflected in a study involving 60 second-grade boys, ages seven and eight years, who played two Nintendo games. One game involved two martial arts heroes who faced ruthless street gangs and aggressively worked their way through various obstacles in order to rescue a friend. The second game was nonaggressive, requiring the player to race a motorcycle against time over various obstacles with no opportunity for a collision with other motorcycles. Boys who had played the aggressive game showed increased physical aggression in their play with peers. They also displayed verbal aggression by describing their behavior as they acted out what they had observed.[26] Other researchers have concluded that the impact of violent video games is greater on very young children as compared to teenagers.[27]

Figure 3.4
Categories of Video Games

1. *Sport Simulations.* This type is self-explanatory. These games simulate sports such as golf, ice hockey, athletics, etc. (e.g., *World Wide Soccer,* '97, *NHL Powerplay* '97, etc).

2. *Racers.* This type could be considered a type of sport simulation in that it simulates motor sports like Formula 1 racing (e.g., *Human Grand Prix, Speedster, Motoracer,* etc.).

3. *Adventures.* This type uses fantasy settings in which the player can escape to other worlds and take on new identities (e.g., *Atlantis, Star Trek Generations, Overboard,* etc.).

4. *Puzzlers.* This type is self-explanatory. These games are "brain-teasers," which often require active thinking (e.g., *Tetris, Baku Baku Animal,* etc.).

5. *Weird Games.* These games are not weird as such except they do not fit into any other category. They would be better termed *miscellaneous* (e.g., *Sin City 2000, Populous 3,* etc.).

6. *Platformers.* These games involve running and jumping along and onto platforms (e.g., *Mario 64, Sonic,* etc.).

7. *Platform Blasters.* These games are platformers but also involve blasting everything that comes into sight (e.g., *Robocop 2, Virtual Cop,* etc.).

8. *Beat 'Em Ups.* These games involve physical violence such as punching and kicking. (e.g., *Street Fighter 3, Tekken 2, Mortal Kombat,* etc.).

9. *Shoot 'Em Ups.* These games involve shooting and killing using various weapons (e.g., *Blast Corps, Mech Warrior, Turok Dinosaur Hunter,* etc).

Reprinted from *Aggression and Violent Behavior,* 4, M. Griffiths, "Violent video games and aggression: A review of the literature," pp. 203-212, 1999, with permission from Elsevier Science.

What About Power and Control?

Patriarchal theory, or the feminist perspective, focuses both on the power and control that males exert over females and the subordinate position in society in which men place women. The term *patriarchy* refers to the father being head of a family or clan over which he dominates, especially its female members. Patriarchy can be seen at the societal level as males dominate the corporate world, government, religious organizations, and society in general. This also occurs at home and in the family, often supported by Christian theology texts taken out of historical and cultural context that are used to encourage women to be submissive to their husbands. In keeping with patriarchal theory, boys are encouraged to assume an active, aggressive position early in their development and girls are taught a more passive, nonassertive role. This can be seen in the types of toys parents buy for their children—trucks and guns for boys, dolls and playing house for girls. Likewise, research indicates that generally in American families, males are more aggressive towards and exert more power and control over females through physical, emotional, or sexual abuse than the other way around.

Figure 3:5

What's Implied in the Question?

Patriarchy can be found in many traditional wedding ceremonies which sets the tone of a family union. In many wedding rites, as the bride reaches the front of the church on her father's arm, the officiant asks, "Who gives this woman to be married to this man?" This part of the ceremony is often referred to as the "giving away of the bride." The question is only asked of the bride's parents, not of the groom's. The question implies that a transfer of property is occurring. At one time cattle, children, and women were viewed as chattel or property belonging to the male.

Just as parts of the wedding ceremony asking the bride to vow that she will "obey" her husband have been removed, so also should the "giving away of the bride" sections be deleted. To avoid patriarchy in the ceremony, the question might be changed to, "Who presents this bride for marriage?" A similar question should then be addressed to the groom's parents, "Who presents this groom for marriage?" Or, as occurs in many European ceremonies, the groom meets the bride at the door of the church and together they come down the aisle followed by each set of parents. The lighting of a unity candle, a popular feature in many wedding ceremonies, then has richer meaning as a new union or family is established through the marriage of the bride and groom.

Two concepts are important in patriarchal theory of aggression: structural power and personal power. Structural or institutionalized power is granted by society to individuals and groups. Individuals and groups use this power to dominate and control others through variables such as gender, race, age, income, and religion. For example, men control women, older siblings hurt younger ones, Caucasians dominate African Americans, and the rich control the poor. Thus, those with little or no structural power can become victims of the misuse of this power through exploitation and aggression.

The abuse of structural power can be checked through the enhancement of personal power—such as inner strength, the desire to attain life mastery, or the drive to achieve personal goals. Some individuals exert control for personal gain with little thought to another's physical or emotional needs. Abuse survivors tend to reflect such violations of personal power. For example, perpetrators of family violence thwart family members from reaching their full human potential by victimizing them, rather than by allowing or assisting their full development. Yet, for the good of all, everyone should be assured the right to be as much as they can.[28]

Why Brother Sister Hurt?

Then why do brothers and sisters physically and emotionally abuse or hurt each other? How do theories of aggression apply to families today? Although later chapters look at specific factors related to sibling abuse, let us now apply, in a general way, the foregoing theories.

First, something should be said about the application of general theories to problem situations. When applying a theory, such as in attempting to understand physical and emotional sibling abuse, one must strive for the theory "of best fit." This means that not every theory will apply. Just as when cooking food one does not use every spice available in the spice rack, but selectively chooses what is best for the particular food being cooked—oregano for tomatoes when making an Italian dish and chili powder for a spicy soup—so one selects theories in terms of which have the best fit.

The biological theory of the four theories of aggression just discussed probably has the poorest fit for our purposes. This is not to deny, however, that it may still be applicable to incidents of physical and emotional sibling abuse. As stated earlier, although there is little empirical support for aggression being a drive or instinct, biological factors can influence aggression. For instance, if adolescents are using drugs and alcohol, they will have less control of aggressive impulses toward siblings. Or, if physical abuse occurs in the context of a rage, seemingly with little provocation, one might suspect a closed-head injury. This is particularly true for adolescent boys who might have been so injured while playing football. However, no children are exempt from such injuries if they have sustained a serious fall or if a head injury has resulted from an automobile accident. If parents are suspicious this may have occurred, consultation with a neurologist is important. A neurologist can determine, through the use of magnetic resonance imagery (MRI), the likelihood of an injury to the brain. Moreover, medication can be prescribed to help a person control aggressive outbursts.

The second theory dealt with aggression resulting from frustration in attaining a goal. In applying this theory to physical and emotional sibling abuse, parents must act as diagnosticians of what is happening to their child. Frustration may be occurring because the child cannot achieve academically or excel in sports like another sibling or peer. Unfortunately, teachers, coaches, and others in authority positions often reinforce the frustration by making comparisons. **The individuality of each child is important. Each child needs to be viewed as a unique individual**. Although two or more children may have been born to the same set of parents, they genetically are unique. This extends even to temperament, abilities, skills, and general personality traits. The parental diagnostic role comes into play in discovering with the child that uniqueness. What sport, if any, might he like to play? What special lessons—music, dance, art— might she like to take? What extracurricular activities does the child want to participate in—chess club, band, cheerleading, scouting? The decision should be made, to a large extent, on the basis of a child's own interests, not on what another sibling is doing or what the parent wants.

The aggression theory that probably has the best fit of all when trying to understand physical and emotional sibling abuse is social learning theory or modeling. A parent should ask, "Where is my child learning to be so physically and emotionally abusive to a sibling?" Because the research indicates that the most abusive siblings come from homes in which parents are abusive to each other, parents need to ask themselves if their child is modeling the behavior they themselves are demonstrating. How do you as parents treat each other? Do you resort to physically aggressive acts such as hitting, slapping, pushing? Do you make degrading comments to each other or use names that are uncomplimentary? And then there are the television, videos, and movies that may consume so much of each family member's time. Is there an "anything goes" policy in terms of what your children can watch on TV or the videos they bring home? What kinds of games are being played on the computer? Do these games center on violent acts? Who are the children's heroes in terms of movie stars, professional athletes, and others in prominent positions? Prescriptions for how parents might handle these issues are given in a later chapter.

Finally, the theory of patriarchy centers of the power and control that males exert over females. What is the relationship of the males and females in your family? Are tasks assigned among family members primarily according to gender—the female children do household tasks such as helping with the cooking, laundry, loading and unloading the dishwasher while the male members take care of the lawn, empty the trash, and do similar tasks? Are female members of the household covertly or not so covertly waiting on or serving the male members? Are expectations for the completion of assigned tasks and consequences for not doing so the same for siblings without regard to gender?

Even though this brief application of aggression theories has occurred on an individual, theory-by-theory basis, in many instances behavior can better be understood when several theories are applied simultaneously. For example, a father telling a "dumb blonde" joke is not only acting as a poor role model to his children but simultaneously is degrading women. In this instance, two theories come into play—social learning theory and the feminist perspective.

Something to Think About

A group of Hollywood writers and producers recently participated in a round-table discussion of their work. At one point in the conversation, the discussion leader asked, "What about the element of violence in the films you produce? A producer quickly responded, "As long as the public demands it by buying it, we will produce it." Others around the table agreed. What do you think? What can you do about violence in films, videos, and TV programs?

Begin to think about aggressive behavior you observe between or among the siblings in your family. Are you able to apply any of the theories discussed in this chapter—biological, frustration, social learning (modeling), power and control—in trying to understand the aggressive behavior of one sibling toward another?

1 Crain, W. (1992). *Theories of development: Concepts and applications* (3rd ed.). Englewood Cliffs, NJ: Prentice Hall.

2 Lorenz, K. (1966). On aggression. New York: Harcourt Brace Jovanovich. Penrod, S. (1986). *Social psychology.* Englewood Cliffs, NJ: Prentice-Hall. Ridley, M. (Ed.). (1987). *The Darwin reader.* New York: Norton.

3 Meyer, D. (1996). *Social psychology* (5th ed.). New York: McGraw-Hill.

4 Eibl-Eibesfeldt, I. (1979). *The biology of peace and war: Men, animals, and aggression.* New York: Viking Press. Nance, J. (1975). *The gentle Tasaday: A stone age people in the Philippine rain forest.* New York: Harcourt Brace Jovanovich.

5 Hornstein, H. (1976). *Cruelty and kindness.* Englewood Cliffs, NJ: Prentice-Hall.

6 Miller, L. (1994). Traumatic brain injury and aggression. *Journal of Offender Services, Counseling, and Rehabilitation,* 21, 91-103. Rosenbaum, A., Hoge, S., Adelman, S., Warnken, W., Fletcher, K., & Kane, R. (1994). Head injury in partner-abusive men. *Journal of Clinical & Consulting Psychology,* 62, 1187-1193.

7 Gustafson, R. (1994). Alcohol and aggression. *Journal of Offender Services, Counseling, and Rehabilitation,* 21, 1-80.

8 Karr-Morse, R., & Wiley, M. (1997). *Ghosts from the nursery: Tracing the roots of violence.* New York: Atlantic Monthly Press.

9 Needleman, H. (1996). Bone lead levels and delinquent behavior. *Journal of the American Medical Association*, 275(5), 363-369.

10 DiLalla, L., & Gottesman, I. (1991). Biological and genetic contributors to violence. Widom's untold tale. *Psychological Bulletin*, 109, 125-129.

11 Wright, R. (1995, March 13). The biology of violence. *The New Yorker*, pp. 68-77.

12 Dollard, J., Doob, L., Miller, N., Mowere, O., & Sears, R. (1939). *Frustration and aggression*. New Haven, CT: Yale University Press. Carlson, M., Marcus-Newhall, A., & Miller, N. (1990). Effects of situational aggression cues: A quantitative review. *Journal of Personality and Social Psychology*, 58, 622-633.

13 Dill, J., & Anderson, C. (1995). Effects of frustration justification on hostile aggression. *Aggressive Behavior*, 21, 359-369.

14 Barker, R., Dembo, T., & Lewin, K. (1941). Frustration and aggression: An experiment with young children. *University of Iowa Studies in Child Welfare*, 18, 1-64.

15 Berkowitz, L. (1978). Whatever happened to the frustration-aggression hypothesis? *American Behavioral Scientist*, 21, 691-708.

16 Berkowitz, L., & LePage, A. (1967). Weapons as aggression-eliciting stimuli. *Journal of Personality and Social Psychology*, 7, 202-207. Turner, C., Simons, L., Berkowitz, L., & Frodi, A. (1977). The stimulating and inhibiting effects of weapons on aggressive behavior. *Aggressive Behavior*, 3, 355-378.

17 Peterson , K. (1998, June 19-21). 1 million school kids toting guns. *USA Today*, pp. A1,A6.

18 Williams, H. (1997), March 26). End the domestic arms race. *The Washington Post*, p. A19.

19 Ibid.

20 Bandura, A., Ross, D., & Ross. S. (1963). Vicarious reinforcement and imitative learning. *Journal of Abnormal and Social Psychology*, 63, 575-582.

21 Weiss, B., Dodge, K., Bates, J., & Pettit, G. (1992). Some consequences of early harsh discipline: Child aggression and a maladaptive social information processing style. *Child Development*, 63, 1321-1335.

22 Bandura, A. (1965). Influence of model's reinforcement contingencies on the acquisition of imitative responses. *Journal of Personality and Social Psychology*, I, 589-595.

23 Pennell, A., & Browne, K. (1999). Film violence and young offenders. *Aggression and Violent Behavior*, 4, 13-28.

24 Phillips, D. (1974). Suicide, motor vehicle fatalities, and the mass media: Evidence toward a theory of suggestion. *American Sociological Review*, 39, 340-354.

25 Phillips, D., & Hensley, J. (1984). When violence is rewarded or punished: The impact of mass media stories on homicide. *Journal of Communication*, 34, 101-116.

26 Irwin, A., & Gross, A. (1995). Cognitive tempo, violent video games, and aggressive behavior in young boys. *Journal of Family Violence*, 10, 337-350.

27 Griffiths, M. (1999). Violent video games and aggression: A review of the literature. *Aggression and Violent Behavior*, 4, 203-212.

28 Walby, C., Clancy, A., Emetchi, J., & Summerfield, C. (1989). Theoretical perspectives on father-daughter incest. In E. Driver & A. Droisen (Eds.), *Child sexual abuse: A feminist reader* (pp. 8-106). New York: New York University Press.

My childhood was a nightmare. My brother was constantly hitting and slapping me. My parents just ignored it.

A sibling abuse survivor

Chapter 4

Recognizing Sibling Physical Abuse

My memories of growing up at home focus on the way my brother who was three years older treated me. He would hit, punch, and slap me continually. If I complained to my parents, they would say, "You must have done something to deserve it" or "Fight your own battles." After a while, I started to fight back, but he was so much bigger and stronger that I couldn't hold my own against him. Besides, then my parents had reason to excuse his actions because they saw me hitting him.

This is the recollection of an adult who as a child was a victim of physical abuse from a sibling. This chapter describes the nature of such abuse. The two subsequent chapters will describe sibling emotional and sexual abuse.

There is very little research about sibling abuse, even though it occurs more frequently than child and partner abuse. Research on sexual abuse in the form of incest is available, but many studies do not identify which family member was the perpetrator (parent, stepparent, grandparent, cousin, or sibling).[1] The information in this book primarily is based on the author's research involving 150 adult survivors of sibling abuse. The following stories portray what survivors experienced at the hands of a sibling and the impact of the physical, emotional, or sexual abuse on their lives.

These accounts are shared to help you recognize sibling abuse that may be occurring with your children. For some of you, the survivors' stories may awaken in you remembrances of having been abused as you were growing up. In either situation, the poignant remarks reported here are not meant to frighten you but rather help you take steps to intervene in any similar behavior in your family. Or, perhaps you will seek professional help if the abuse you experienced as a child is creating problems-in-living for you as an adult. In some instances, the accounts are very drastic: in others, the behavior is not so severe. As will be discussed later, the severity of the behavior is not the only factor determining if and when a parent should intervene. Most important is usually the *pattern* of abuse occurring over time or, in instances of sexual abuse, even the awareness of a single incident.

What Is Physical Abuse?

Sibling physical abuse can take many forms. Research participants who reported being physically abused by a sibling can be grouped into three categories: 1) most common forms of physical abuse; 2) unusual forms; and, 3) injurious or life-threatening forms. The personal stories of adult survivors relate the way these various forms of abuse occurred.

Most common forms. Survivors most often reported the following physical abuse: hitting, slapping, shoving, punching, biting, hair pulling, scratching, and pinching. Other forms of sibling physical abuse which parents should be aware of include poking, strangling, bending fingers back, and beating. Survivors also were hit with objects such as broom handles, rubber hoses, coat hangers, hair brushes, belts, and sticks. They were threatened and stabbed with broken glass, knives, razor blades, and scissors. To this we must now add being threatened with a gun because of the availability of such weapons and their presence in so many American homes.

A woman described her memories of physical abuse by her brother:

When I was three or four, my brother pushed me down some stone steps. I had approximately thirty stitches in my knee. As I grew older, my brother typically would slug me in the arm, push me down on the floor, and hold me down while he would hit me in the stomach. I was not to cry or my parents would make us go to our rooms, and then I would be in bigger trouble with my brother.

One survivor told of her abuse from an older brother:

He would engage me in wrestling matches daily, typically punching me in the stomach until I could not breathe, torturing my wrist and knee joints, spitting on me, putting his knees on my arms, and pinning me down and beating on my chest with his knuckles.

A respondent revealed the physical abuse he had received from an older brother and its source.

Usually the abuse would consist of getting beat up by my brother with his fists or being slapped around with the inside of his hands, a practice he learned from our parents, along with being kicked in the rear.

A respondent retains this vivid memory of the childhood abuse she suffered from two older brothers:

I remember frequently being curled up in a living room chair with my hands over my face being hit over and over. I usually ended up on the floor and not moving or making noises so my brother would go away.

Another survivor wrote:

My sister would hit, kick, or spit on me. Although she was only one year older, she was always much stronger and bigger than me.

Often the abuse escalated as this survivor described:

The abuse consisted usually of my brother punching me in the arms, stomach, back, etc. Usually it started out with a verbal fight, but sometimes he just began punching me if I wouldn't do what he told me to or if he wanted to watch something different on TV. Sometimes things were worse. Once he tried to hit me with an aluminum baseball bat. When I ran away and locked myself in the bathroom, he kicked a hole in the door.

Another survivor described what he experienced and a reaction that is probably typical of many siblings at the time they are abused; namely, they don't realize that what is happening is abuse:

A minor argument would erupt into violence when I wouldn't do what my brother wanted me to or I wouldn't agree with his opinion. I was shaken, hit, kicked, and slapped. I was never badly hurt, but the level of my brother's rage was such that I was always afraid of it. I knew what was happening was wrong, but I don't think I thought of it as abuse at the time. I have blocked out my memories of these events for many years and still do not have all of them back.

An unusual form. Although generally not regarded as abusive, tickling can in fact become so. Tickling can be pleasant, even erotic, or it can be painful. That is, the nerve fibers that respond to tickling are the same ones that respond to pain. Tickling can be pleasant when there is trust and mutual respect. In such a context, a person trusts that the behavior will stop upon request.

But tickling becomes painful if the person has no control over the situation. When a child requests that the tickling cease and it does not, this behavior is abusive. As survivors reported, some perpetrators even restrained their victims, such as pinning them to the floor. Often, there was little the victims could do because they were smaller or weaker than their siblings.

Several survivors described having serious reactions to the tickling. One woman said that her sister, three years older, would punch, slap, and pin her to the floor—sometimes until she would vomit.

Another survivor reported:

I was unmercifully tickled by my brother who held down every limb and body part that wiggled and who covered my mouth when I cried and yelled for help. He pulled my hair after I pulled his, thinking that would hurt him and he would stop.

This woman's mother ignored what her brother did, calling it playing, even though she tried to convince her mother otherwise. This abuse affects her even now as an adult. She does not like to be touched, especially when people hug her or hold her in any way reminiscent of being restrained.

A survivor described a similar reaction from her mother when she mentioned the abuse she was experiencing from two siblings:

My brother and sister would hold me down and tickle me until I cried. They considered this play and would usually do it when my parents were gone. They would finally let me go and then laugh because I was a "crybaby."

Injurious or life-threatening forms. Play among siblings sometimes escalates into aggressive behavior and can result in injury. All children probably at some time or another are injured while playing, even accidentally, by a sibling. Survivors reported incidents in which siblings shot them with BB guns, attempted to drown them, smothered them under pillows until they nearly suffocated (in one instance needing mouth-to-mouth resuscitation), and repeatedly hit them in the stomach until they lost their breath.

Following are some extreme examples that survivors described:

My brother discovered that hitting in the solar plexus caused one to black out. So he would hit me and watch me pass out.

* * *

My oldest brother would put his arms around my chest tight and not let me inhale any air while I had to watch in the mirror as he laughed and explained how I was going to die.

* * *

If ever my brother found me sleeping in my sleeping bag, he would force me to the bottom of the bag and hold the top closed so I couldn't get out or breathe. When I realized I couldn't get out, I would become panic-stricken and think I was going to die. Even as I write this, I am taken back to that moment and feel just the way I felt then. As an adult, I'm claustrophobic and can't have my face covered without panic setting in.

* * *

I don't remember when it started but my brothers and sisters used to hit me in the stomach to knock the breath out of me because I had asthma and they thought it was funny to see me wheeze. I was around four or five years old. Also, my sister and brothers would hit me in the nose to make me sneeze and count the number of times I would sneeze. Whoever made me sneeze most was the winner. Once I sneezed seventeen times. On another occasion, I bled all over a new chair my parents had bought after my brother had hit me in the nose. I was punished by my parents for doing so.

How are these incidents different from ordinary play that results in injury? First, **the experiences occurred frequently**. They were not isolated events. For the survivors, the abuse was typical of the behavior they experienced from a sibling.

Second, **the perpetrator's reaction to the victim's injury was hurtful**. In most cases, the perpetrator laughed at the victim. This reaction added further "injury" by giving the message that the behavior had somehow been intentional.

Third, **the parents' reaction was not appropriate.**

Usually, parents comfort injured children, take care of their injuries, and punish a child who is aggressive. At the very least, parents make an attempt to determine what happened. But when parents react to an injurious or life-threatening incident with nonchalance, denial of the suffering experienced, or even blaming the victim for what happened, the incident becomes abusive.

One woman related several of many physically abusive incidents by her sister. The scars from some of these injuries remain today as a reminder of the physical abuse she experienced as a child:

When I was about four, I climbed on the chicken coop and a nail penetrated my foot. It went all the way through my foot. I was literally nailed to the coop. My sister saw me and laughed and told me that's what I deserved. She left me and wouldn't help me down. After a long time, my older brother came by and helped me get down and took me to the hospital. On another occasion, when I was about five years old and my sister was a teenager, she was ironing and I was curious as to what she was doing. I put my hands flat up on the ironing board and she immediately put the hot iron down on my hand. She laughed. I still have the burn scar on my left hand.

A woman remembered the injurious abuse she had suffered from an older brother and her parents' response:

When I was two or three, my mother went to visit my father who was in the Army, and my brother and I were left in the care of my grandparents. My brother was helping my grandfather paint a fence, and he painted me from head to toe with dark brown paint. I remember the paint was in my hair, face, clothing, etc., and I had to be scrubbed down with turpentine and repeated baths. Some of my hair had to be cut to get the paint out. My brother laughed and teased me about this. Later, during another incident, my brother wrote his name on my bare back with his woodburning kit. He seemed to treat me as an object rather than as a person with any feelings. My abuse continued through high school. My brother would twist my arms or pin me down and bend my arms or legs to get me to do things he wanted me to do, such as his chores or to cover for him by lying to my parents. These incidents usually happened when my parents weren't home. When I reported them to my parents, he would say I was making it up to get him into trouble. Then we would both be punished. I knew my parents didn't know how to handle the problem, so I quit reporting to them. I would just arrange to go to a friend's house or have a friend over when my parents were going to be out.

"I have photographs of my brother pushing me down and trying to 'playfully' strangle me when I was an infant," said one woman. When she was four or five years old, her brother would hold her down and, in a threatening but supposedly playful manner, put his hands around her neck as if to choke her to death. To this day, she remains frightened of men and has a phobia about anyone touching her neck. Because of her experiences with her sibling, she is not willing to have more than one child.

Respondents told of being smothered with a pillow, another form of life-threatening physical abuse. Although youngsters at play often tussle, this activity on a couch or bed can quickly turn abusive. The frightened response of one child can even become a cue for the sibling to demonstrate more power and control.

I remember my brother putting a pillow over my head. He would hold it and laugh while I struggled to get out from under him and the pillow. I remember being terrified. I honestly thought he would smother me to death. This occurred frequently.

Something to Think About

What behaviors do your siblings engage in together that one or the other does not like or that you find irritating and offensive? Do the behaviors fall under one of the three categories of physical abuse described in this chapter?

1 See, for example, Wiehe, V. (1997). *Sibling abuse: Hidden physical, emotional, and sexual trauma* (2nd ed.). Thousand Oaks, CA: Sage. This book reports the results of a study involving 150 adults who were seeking help for problems in living from mental health centers and therapists in private practice. The subjects responded to a 14 page questionnaire in which they were asked to describe the nature of the abuse they experienced from a sibling, their parents response to the abuse, the way in which the abuse has impacted on their psychosocial functioning, and their suggestions for preventing sibling abuse in families.

My sister seemed to take delight in calling me names and making degrading comments about me, even in front of my friends.

A sibling abuse survivor

Chapter 5

Recognizing Emotional Abuse

When I was in grade school, I was somewhat overweight. My older sister started to call me "Lardo." After a while, my younger brother picked up on the name. My weight was a frequent topic of discussion in our family. My parents would say things like, "You have such a pretty face, if only you got rid of that extra weight" and "No one is going to date you when you are fat."

One time my older sister called me "Lardo" at school in front of some of my friends. Everyone laughed. I wanted to cry. That evening I told my mother what had happened and her response was that I deserved it if I didn't lose weight. I was very hurt by what she said. She doesn't know it, but I even thought of committing suicide. I am now twenty three years old, single, and working as a secretary. The emotional abuse I experienced from my sibling, which my parents would not stop, has left me a "loner." I go to my job, go home, and stay in my apartment. I'm thinking of joining a support group for overweight people as a way to deal with my low self-esteem.

What Is Emotional Abuse?

"Sticks and stones may break my bones, but words will never hurt me." Children bravely mouth this familiar jingle in the face of persecution by other children. Although physical abuse may leave bruises and other evidence, emotional abuse leaves no outward marks. However, the jingle is very incorrect when it boasts that words, the basic component of emotional abuse, do not hurt.

In the author's research, individuals who identified themselves as victims of emotional abuse or psychological maltreatment by a sibling often said they were teased. Teasing is not only a common behavior but also a catch-all word for a number of similar acts. Teasers frequently hurt others when they belittle, intimidate, annoy, scorn or provoke.

Researchers in the field of child abuse suggest that emotional abuse is more prevalent and potentially more destructive than other forms of child abuse and typically under-lies physical and sexual abuse.[1] This is equally true in sibling relationships. Generally, emotional abuse includes the following behaviors: name-calling, ridicule, degradation, rejecting, terror-izing, isolating, corrupting, the destruction of personal possessions, and the torture or destruction of a pet.

Emotional abuse, however, is difficult to identify. Because emotional abuse leaves no physical evidence, to an outside observer a family might appear to be operating well, but at home one child is emotionally abusing another. In addition, accepted legal standards are not available for proving that emotional or behavioral problems resulted from emotional abuse or for deter-mining the seriousness of emotional abuse. Detecting such abuse is complicated by the fact that professionals and parents have regarded this behavior as "normal" for children's interac-tions among siblings and peers. Teasing and verbal put-downs of brothers and sisters, although disliked by parents, are simply excused as sibling rivalry.

When parents excuse or overlook emotional abuse in the family, however, victims get the message that this behavior is really not abusive. In fact, some child-rearing practices and family cultural values actually reinforce denial that certain interactions are abusive. For example, a parent may call a child "slob" who has a messy room. Or, a parent may even make derogatory remarks about a child who is overweight. These comments supposedly are made to motivate the child to change the dysfunctional behavior—to keep a cleaner room or to watch caloric intake, however, they have the opposite effect on a child. The comments destroy the child's self-esteem and often only make matters worse. Adult survivors of sibling abuse report that emotional abuse in the form of name-calling, ridicule, and degradation was a common pattern in their lives when they were growing up—from their siblings and even sometimes from their parents. Adult sibling abuse survivors repeatedly use words like constant and always in describing their childhood spent in a climate of mockery:

I was constantly being told by an older sibling that I was no good, a pig, whore, slut—all sexually oriented negatives. Even my parents degraded me at times.

* * *

I can't remember a time when I was growing up when my brother didn't taunt me.

* * *

From my earliest memories, age five or so, my siblings called me names and said degrading things to me.

Historically, children have been physically abused by adults who viewed them as property. What occurred behind closed doors of the family residence was considered the family's private business.[2] Children who experienced severe beatings were forced to conclude that they deserved this behavior, despite their physical and emotional suffering. Within the past several decades as society has recognized the social consequences of adult-child physical abuse, victims have been encouraged to seek help. Likewise, until all sibling abuse is recognized for what it is, survivors are at risk to believe that this is normal behavior, to accept that they deserve such treatment, and—most tragic of all—to pass on its effects to their children.

The challenge to protect siblings from abuse increases when one realizes the extensive web of destruction presented by the interaction of emotional, physical, and sexual abuse. Emotional abuse that interacts with physical abuse is demonstrated by the following comments of a survivor of abuse from a brother three years older than she:

I can't remember a time when my brother didn't taunt me, usually trying to get me to respond so he would be justified in hitting me. Usually he would be saying I was a crybaby or a sissy or stupid or ugly and that no one would like me, want to be around me, or whatever. Sometimes he would accuse me of doing something, and if I denied it, then he would call me a liar. I usually felt overwhelmingly helpless because nothing I said or did would stop him. If no one else was around, he would start beating on me after which he would stop and go away. I felt helpless to stop any of it.

Another survivor described how her brother, nine years older, used emotional abuse in connection with sexual abuse.

The sexual abuse stemmed directly from the emotional abuse. The earliest memory was when I was about five years old. It is difficult for me to be specific about a single event because I've blocked a lot out of my mind. But I was always afraid of being rejected by my parents. My brother was the oldest and he made me believe that my parents would always believe him over me because I was only 5 and he was thirteen. So, you see, he always had some sort of power over me emotionally and physically. As a child and adolescent, I was introverted and never really shared my inner feelings with anyone. I felt like dirt and that my needs, concerns, and opinions never mattered, only those of other people. I was always in fear of both forms of abuse (emotional and sexual). I learned to prepare myself for both. I'm so resentful that I had to do this to survive mentally in my home. My brother would always present himself in these situations as being perfect, mature, responsible, brave—a model brother. Then, I'd feel like an immature, non-credible child. He'd say things like how my parents thought he was so special, being the oldest. And, that if I told on him, I would destroy the entire family; my parents would divorce; I would be sent to a foster home. He had such emotional control over me in that sense that I "obeyed" him and never told. He had control over my self-image and my body.

How Will I Know It Is Abuse?

Emotional abuse is so common in some families that it is difficult for parents to even know when such abuse is occurring.

Name-calling. Perpetrators appear to use name-calling as an easy way to belittle or degrade their siblings. The name-calling generally focuses on some attribute, such as the victim's height, weight, physical characteristics, intelligence, or inability to perform a skill. Adult survivors recall experiences with name-calling:

When I was six, my mother realized I needed glasses. For the next several years my brother told me I was ugly and taunted me with a lot of names referring to being unattractive.

* * *

I was heavy as a young child, about seven or eight years old. My brother called me, "Cow." He was asked to mark all the children's socks with our names so for mine he drew the face of a cow. He called me a Spanish word which I later understood meant "whore."

* * *

My sister would verbally harass me—you're ugly, stupid, fat, etc. If I did accomplish anything, she would turn things around and prove that I had failed or had been a fool.

Ridicule. Ridicule appears to be a sport to some siblings. Several survivors relived the painful motions that accompanied actions—even laughter—to express contempt:

My sister would get her friends to sing songs about how ugly I was.

* * *

Life as a child consisted of constant taunts and ridicule on issues, such as the things I said, the clothes I wore, my friends, etc.

* * *

I was ridiculed by my older brothers and sisters for just being. Ridicule and put-downs were "normal" for our family.

Degradation. "You're worthless and no good." Attacks on one's dignity and worth are emotionally devastating to victims both at the time the abuse occurs and even later as adults. Survivors indicated that degrading messages from a brother or sister continue to haunt them, often becoming a self-fulfilling prophecy. This is especially true for those whose parents did not intervene in the abusive behavior but ignored it, accepted it as normal, or worst of all, participated in it.

The childhood years are intended for developing a positive sense of self-worth and self-esteem. Negative interactions with peers in play and at school, however, can negate this opportunity. Verbal put-downs between siblings (and peers) occur so frequently that parents and others in authority tend to accept them as normal. To make matters worse, children may react by appearing as if the degrading comments have no effect—the stoical reaction perhaps at the root of the "sticks and stones" jingle. But in taking a defensive stance, victims deny their emotional pain. Unfortunately, however, this reaction usually reinforces or encourages the perpetrator. The behavior, therefore, can be expected to continue unless some action is taken by adults to discontinue it. This is why it is so important for parents to be aware of emotional abuse and to stop it when it is occurring.

Many respondents said that their emotional abuse followed them into adulthood. "Labeling theory" explains that one child in a family may be targeted as the scapegoat or as outside the family circle. Childhood nicknames and labels given by siblings, often focusing on a specific personality trait or physical characteristic, remain with them as adults:

I was being constantly told how ugly, dumb, unwanted I was. At an early age, I was told, "No one wants you around. I [my sister] wish you were dead. You aren't my real sister, your parents didn't want you, either, so they dumped you with us." I grew up feeling, if my own family doesn't like me, who will? I believed everything my sister ever told me—that I was ugly, dumb, homely, stupid, fat—even though I always was average in weight. I felt no one would ever love me. When you're little, you believe everything you're told. It can last a lifetime.

Survivors who experienced emotional abuse in the form of degradation reported having a pervasive feeling during childhood that they should not exist. The transactional analysis (TA) school of psychology, popular some years ago in the book *I'm OK, You're OK* by Eric Berne, refers to this as "Don't Be," a "game" some parents even engage in with a child. A subtle message is given in a variety of ways that life would be much better if the child were not around. The parents would have fewer financial expenses or there would be less tension in the home. This destructive behavior is also used by siblings against one another. Although a child is not responsible for his or her existence, the "game" carries an underlying wish for the child's destruction.

My brothers loved to tease me to tears. They were ruthless in their teasing and did not let up. They teased me for being ugly. They teased me for being sloppy. They teased me for just being. This was the worst.

Another form of degradation, especially by older children toward younger siblings and by brothers toward sisters, is to "use" the sibling. In the survey, sisters described their brothers as "lording it over" them. A brother would command his sister to do things such as household chores that he was expected to do. Failure to comply with the perpetrator's demands at times resulted in physical abuse. In essence, the brother would exert power and control over his sister.

Recall the feminist perspective of aggression with the themes of power and control discussed in an earlier chapter. A survivor who was raised on a farm in the Midwest in a very religious family of eight children provided an example of this. She had to wait on her older brothers in the house, even if she had been working all day in the fields. Her parents had instructed her to obey her older brothers in their absence. "It was as if my brothers could do no wrong." The older brothers took advantage of her, not only by demanding that she do tasks for them but also by tricking her out of her allowance and eventually sexually abusing her.

Playing on a fear. Older siblings often take advantage of a younger child who is afraid of being lost, of the dark, or of strangers. Perpetrators in the study used fear as a means of exerting power and control over the siblings thereby getting them to do what they wanted. Perhaps the children were modeling their parents who also used fear to coerce their children. The following comments are by survivors:

My older siblings would take my sister and me out into the field to pick berries. When we would hear dogs barking, they would tell us there were wild dogs, and then they'd run away and make us find our own way home. We were only five or six and we didn't know our way home.

* * *

I remember very clearly that my older sister, who was seven years older, would go to the telephone and pretend to call a man she called, "Mr. Krantz." He ran an institution, she said, for "bad children" and she threatened sending me there, banishing me from the family. I was terrified.

One survivor wrote that an older sister played upon her fear of the dark to force her to do the older sister's household tasks and in general to control her. The victim was afraid of the dark, but her older sister would allow her to sleep with her as long as she did everything her older sister demanded. The victim was caught in a bind. If she told her parents about it, she would be banished from sleeping with her sister. Thus, she would be alone with her fear of the dark. The survivor indicated that she acquiesced to her sister's control and repeatedly became the victim of her emotional abuse.

Destroying personal possessions. A child's possessions, such as a bicycle, toys, or clothing, are especially valued. Everyone remembers a favorite toy, book, or blanket from their childhood. Some adults may still have these objects. Yet, even when a perpetrator destroys a sibling's prized object, the actual target of the abuse is the brother or sister. Thus, harming the object is actually harming the individual who treasures the object.

One participant related how as a small child he experienced this form of emotional abuse from an older brother, who deliberately broke his treasured Mickey Mouse ears—and then laughed about it. Initially, this seems humorous. Why should an adult care about his older brother doing that so many years ago?

To understand and empathize with the victim, several factors must be considered. First, the destructive behavior was only one in a series of continual abusive incidents directed at the victim. (A single abusive incident, nevertheless, may be just as harmful, such as sexual molestation by a sibling.) That is, the destruction of the toy per se is not the point.

Second, this destructive behavior must be viewed in the context of the deliberateness of the perpetrator's action. Victims repeatedly wrote of the delight that siblings took in destroying something that was meaningful to them. The incident was not an accident; the intent to harm made it abusive.

Third, the incident must be considered in light of its impact on the victim. The respondent was deeply hurt by his brother's behavior; he, not the toy, was the real target. The statement often made when something like this happens is: "How could someone do this to **me**!"

Survivors gave other examples of emotional abuse through the destruction of personal possessions:

My sister would take my things and wreck them, cut my clothes up to fit her, and blackmail me to do her housework.

* * *

My brother would cut off the eyes, ears, mouth, and fingers of my dolls and hand them to me.

Harming a pet. Although the torture or destruction of a pet may resemble the destruction of prized possessions, it involves the abuse of life, an animal's life. This implies an even greater degree of cruelty toward the object, and just as much or more emotional pain for the sibling.

Survivors reported the following examples:

My second-oldest brother shot my little dog that I loved dearly. It loved me, only me. I cried by its grave for several days. Twenty years passed before I could care for another dog.

* * *

My older brother would come into my room and tear up my toys. He would beat my dog after tying his legs together and wrapping a cloth around its mouth to tie it shut. My brother would tell me I was stupid and say, "Why me, why me; Why did I get a sister so stupid and dumb?" My brother also would tell me he hated me and wished I were dead.

Something to Think About

How does one sibling in your family "get under the skin of" or irritate another sibling?

At home, do you observe that a pattern of behavior has been established?

What is your reaction when this occurs?

1 Garbarino, J., Guttman, E., & Seeley, J. (1986). *The psychologically battered child.* San Francisco: Jossey-Bass. Hart, S., & Brassard, M. (1987). A major threat to children's mental health – psychological maltreatment. *American Psychologists*, 42, 160-165.

2 See, for example, DeMause, L. (1974). *A history of childhood.* New York: Psychotherapy Press.

My brother, two years older, would commonly grab my chest when my breasts were developing and would twist. When I asked him to stop, he would say, "You love it and you know it."

A sibling abuse survivor

Chapter 6

What Is Sexual Abuse?

When I was about seven years old, my brother who was fourteen told me he wanted to teach me something. He would baby-sit me in the evening while my mother worked. My parents were divorced and, because my Dad never paid child support, my mother had to work two jobs. My brother took his pants down and showed me his erect penis. He proceeded to tell me what adults do when they have sex and touched my vaginal area. He warned me that if I ever told our mother about this, he would kill me. His sexual abuse of me increased with time. He never would penetrate me but he often would come into my bedroom when I had just gone to bed, lay on top of me, and rub back and forth simulating intercourse. Then he would masturbate. I was too scared to tell my mother because my brother was a bully, and I didn't know what he might do to me.

Sexual abuse may be thought of only as being forced intercourse—rape. However, a more inclusive definition needs to be used. The feminist perspective, for example, uses a broader definition that refers to both contact and non-contact forms. Contact forms include touching, fondling, attempted penetration, intercourse, rape, or sodomy. Noncontact forms include exhibitionism, forcing a sibling to observe sexual behavior, taking pornographic pictures of a sibling, voyeurism, sexual propositions, and harassment.

How Does the Abuse Begin?

Most survivors could remember the earliest incident of sexual abuse by a sibling as occurring when they were five to seven years old. However, their sexual abuse may actually have begun at a much earlier age than they could recall. Some survivors reported being aware that they had been sexually abused as infants, but they did not indicate how they became aware of this.

Statistical data are not available specifically for sibling sexual abuse of very small children because this frequently occurs "behind the closed doors" of the family home and is kept a secret unless medical help is sought. Nevertheless, such abuse does happen. On the other hand, we do have statistical information on adult-child sexual abuse that reveals incidents of sexual abuse already for children in infancy. Abuse at this age is usually discovered when a child is taken to an emergency room for vaginal bleeding or tearing. An investigation by a protective service agency confirms the abuse often perpetrated by a mother's boyfriend. The child may not retain the incident in her conscious memory; however, this does not detract from the seriousness of such abuse.

Parents often think of children engaging in sexual activity only when they reach adolescence or become sexually mature, not at age four, five or even younger. Surely, children are not interested in or knowledgeable about sex at such an early age, they rationalize. But, a child can become a victim of sexual abuse at any age.

In most incidents of sibling sexual abuse, survivors report that the perpetrator was generally three to ten years older than the victim. This might not have happened, however, if parents had provided the younger child with information about preventing sexual abuse, such as to forcefully say no and to report the incident immediately to them regardless of any threats made by the perpetrator.

Survivors described their earlier memories of sexual abuse:

I was four years old and my older brother told me that he wanted to show me something that Mom and Dad did. I refused. Then he offered to pay me a quarter and said that I would like it. If I turned him down, it was clear that he would hurt me. So I gave in and he made me perform oral sex on him.

* * *

My brother threatened to kill me if I told our parents about him molesting me. I was three or four years of age at the time; he was about 18. He showed me the butcher block we kept in the cellar with the ax and blood for butchering chickens. He said he'd kill me there if I told.

* * *

My earliest memory is when I was 10 and my brother was thirteen. He came into my bed while we were on vacation and were sharing a bedroom. This happened while my parents were out on the town. I pretended I was asleep, and it was very difficult to determine what to do about it because of the physical pleasure I experienced.

When Is It Just Curiosity?

Is any contact of a sexual nature between siblings sexual abuse? Not necessarily. Some contacts may be described as sexual curiosity. All children explore their bodies and may engage in visual or even manual investigation of a sibling's body. This is one way children discover sexual differences or verify what parents have told them. Two small children exploring each other's bodies does not predestine them to a life of emotional chaos and suffering. For example, four-year-old Todd was observed by a nursery school attendant showing his penis to Haley, who was the same age. When the children became aware that the teachers had seen their behavior, Todd's reaction was to blame Haley, saying she had asked him to do this. Haley denied it. The teacher later took the children aside and talked about their sexuality at a level they could understand. This was an opportunity to review with them an earlier class discussion on the subject of "good touches" and "secret touches."

Sexual activity may be viewed relative to the age and emotional developmental level of a child. Preschool-age children (ages 0-5) are intensely curious to explore their universe. This may be expressed in the sexual behaviors of masturbation and looking at others' bodies. Children in primary school (ages 6-10) like to play games with peers and continue to examine their universe. Sexual behaviors may include masturbation, looking at others' bodies, sexual exposure of themselves to others, and even sexual fondling of peers or younger children in a play or game-like atmosphere.

Among preadolescent children (ages 10-12) and adolescents (ages 13-17), behaviors focus on individuation, such as separation from parents and family and developing relationships with peers. Among adolescents, this includes practicing intimacy with peers of the same or other sex. Sexual behavior for these developmental stages include masturbation, an intense interest in voyeuristic activities involving viewing others' bodies through pictures, films, or videos (some of which may be pornographic), or attempts at "peeking" in other-sex locker/dressing rooms. At these ages, open-mouth kissing, sexual fondling, simulated intercourse, and intercourse involving penetration are common sexual activities.[1]

Sexual activity among consenting participants probably presents the least risk of unfavorable consequences. However, a word of caution is in order. Young children who appear to consent actually do not because they cannot anticipate unfavorable consequences from their behavior. In many instances, what appears to be consent may actually be only passive consent, or the inability to make a rational decision because of limited cognitive skills and life experiences.

One factor affecting children's emotional development is the range of societal attitudes toward sexuality demonstrated by parents. Some adults are very uncomfortable with sexual issues, pretending this area of life does not exist. At the other end of the continuum, some advocate open sexual activity in the presence of children and even encourage children to engage in sexual activity. Neither approach guarantees healthy sexual development.

Because of the effect of sexual abuse by an adult, a peer, or a sibling on a child's later adult psychosocial functioning, it is important for parents to take a proactive approach to sexuality by providing their children with developmentally appropriate information and a home atmosphere where sexual concerns and problems can be discussed.

Typical Experiences

Sibling physical and emotional abuse often continues and proceeds to different kinds of sexual abuse, often still accompanied by physical and emotional abuse. The repetitious nature of these incidents often happen to children who are victims of sexual assault by an adult male, such as their father or another family member. The sexual assault generally continues until the child is old enough to forcibly prohibit it or until the behavior is discovered and appropriate interventions occur. Only a few survivors reported that their sexual experience with a sibling was a one-time event.

Siblings typically said that their perpetrators had voiced *threats of harm or even death* if they told their parents. For example, an older brother may threaten to harm his younger sister if she refuses to engage in sexual activity with him. This is a significant way in which sibling sexual abuse differs from adult-child abuse. Adult perpetrators usually tell their victims that they are special and that the sexual activity will be a secret they alone share. Threats of harm may occur, although most often the child victim of an adult becomes entrapped in the perpetrator's web of abuse through enticement, not threats.

Several respondents mentioned the progressive nature of their sexual abuse by an older sibling:

I can't remember exactly how the sexual abuse started, but when I was smaller there was a lot of experimenting. He would do things to me like putting his finger in my vagina. Then, as I got older, he would perform oral sex on me.

* * *

Initially, I was forced to masturbate him one night, but from then on it moved quickly to oral sex on him and, eventually, rape.

Clarification should be made about the use of the term rape. In most states, *rape* is legally defined as the penetration of the penis into the vagina under force or threat of force. On the basis of a growing understanding of sexual abuse and its effect on victims, *rape* is now being defined more broadly, consistent with feminist thought. Thus, as indicated in the opening of this chapter, it may refer to any sexual activity—contact or noncontact—between a perpetrator and a victim in which force, the threat of force, or threats in general are used. An example of the latter is a warning from the perpetrator not to tell anyone because "of what might happen."

The more inclusive meaning of the term *rape* has important implications for both the prosecution of perpetrators and the treatment of victims. On the one hand, a perpetrator's use of aggression, force, or threats makes him or her liable for prosecution of rape regardless of the nature of the activity. That is, fondling a victim's genitals can no longer be labeled less harmful than sexual intercourse because the consequences are the same: The victim's right to privacy has been abused by means of an aggressive act—rape. On the other hand, victims may need treatment in the aftermath of sexually aggressive acts regardless of the nature of the activity. The respondent quoted earlier used the word *rape* in the legal sense: sexual intercourse under force or the threat of force. Actually, she had already become a victim of rape after being required to engage in masturbation and oral sex against her wishes.

Other survivors also were violated—raped—in this way by a sibling:

It began as games and grew to "look and feel." I did not want to do this, but he would threaten me. He was bigger and I was scared. As I became older, he played with my breasts and then fondled my genitals. All this he did against my wishes.

* * *

I would try to put off going to bed. I would try to cover up tight with my blankets. My brother would come into my room and touch me all over. I would tell him to stop, but he would just ignore me. Sometimes, I would pretend I was asleep. After he would leave, I'd cry and cry. I often thought to myself, how can I stop him from doing this to me. But it continued to go on.

Sibling sexual abuse can occur in any type of family, regardless of socioeconomic status. The following comment is by a survivor whose mother had completed several years of college, and the father held a graduate degree from a university:

It became much more frequent as my brother got older. It mostly happened when I was in sixth to ninth grade, ages eleven to fifteen. I knew he would try, so I would lock myself in my room. He would pick the lock and force me to the floor or bed. I can remember yelling at him, or crying, or begging. I tried everything I could think of, for example, appealing to his morals as a brother. I kept a calendar during his senior year of high school. I had made it a "countdown" of when he'd move out upon graduation with the numbers going down.

Commonly, perpetrators isolated the victim in order for the sexual abuse to occur. One respondent told how her older brother would know just when to attack her:

He would always seem to know when I was alone and when no one could hear. I would always know when he had entered a room and when it would happen. He would make me terrified. I would think, "Oh, no, not again!" He'd try to compliment me in a sexual way. Complimenting a four- to six-year-old on her "great breasts" was not what I'd call a turn-on. He would make me touch his erection. I hated that because he'd force me to do it and would hold my hand against it to almost masturbate him. He never orgasmed, though. He'd touch me, almost like he was examining me. He attempted intercourse, but that was difficult. He'd force my legs apart. I was always so scared because my muscles were so tight and my opening was so small. He never really could enter without severe pain. I would say he was hurting me, which he was, and I'd cry in hopes he'd stop. Sometime he did. Other times, he would force himself inside of me so that I would hurt for days.

Although most of the survivors were women, the following comments are from a man:

My brother caught me masturbating once. That's when the sexual abuse began. At night, he would have me fondle him, masturbate him, and fellate him, depending on what he wanted. He threatened to tell Mom about catching me masturbating if I didn't go along. The abuse went on about a year or two. It was always at night. He would lie on his back. A street light would shine across his body through the curtains, and he would call me to come "do" him. I felt like I was on stage with the street light and trapped in a bad part. I hated him immensely. Finally, after a year or so, I told him he could tell whomever he wanted, but I wouldn't do it anymore. The abuse stopped, but the damage was done. My feelings would haunt me into high school, college, and my marriage.

Something to Think About

What ages are your children? What sexual behaviors might they be expected to engage in?

Have you observed sexual activity between your children or with their peers? Are they knowledgeable about sex relative to their developmental age?

1 Sgroi, S., Bunk, B., & Wabrek, C. (1988). Children's sexual behaviors and their relationship to sexual abuse. In S. Sgroi (Ed.), *Vulnerable populations* (Vol. 1, p. 137-186). Lexington, MA: Lexington Books.

I think I spent my childhood hiding from my brother who physically and emotionally abused me. The worst was when he began to sexually abuse me. I lived in fear of him.

A sibling abuse survivor

Chapter 7

How Do Children Cope With Sibling Abuse?

It is important for parents to be aware of the ways in which children cope with physical, emotional, and sexual abuse from a sibling. Certain behaviors may be indicators of the type and degree of abuse a child is experiencing. Adult sibling abuse survivors report similar ways in which they coped as children with physical and emotional abuse from a sibling; however, different coping mechanisms were used when there was sexual abuse. Therefore, the coping mechanisms for physical and emotional abuse are presented together. Again, examples from adult survivors of sibling abuse will be used to illustrate the various ways survivors coped as a child when abused by a sibling.

Coping with Physical and Emotional Abuse

Protecting themselves. As one would expect, most victims attempted in whatever ways possible to protect themselves. A young woman from New York said: "My sister who was a year older would beat me up, and I would sit on my bed with my knees up guarding myself until she stopped."

Screaming and crying. Another natural reaction was to

scream or cry out for help. Unfortunately, this often provoked the perpetrator to intensify the abuse. Here is a common scenario: An older brother is beating on a younger sister. If the younger child calls for help, the beating intensifies under the warning, "Take it like you should!" or "If you cry, I'll give you more." Be aware that the perpetrator, like all children, may be modeling this behavior from a parent or other adults. For example, a parent may be punishing a child by spanking. Afterward, the parent warns, "If you don't stop crying, I'll really give you something to cry about."

Separating themselves from the perpetrator. Victims in positions of powerlessness vis-a-vis siblings who were older and stronger responded the only way they could—separating themselves. At times, they literally would hide in order to avoid being abused. The victims would lock themselves in their bedrooms, if they were fortunate enough to have their own room, or spend as much time as possible away from home with friends. Victims appeared to live in constant fear of further abuse, always having to sense the mood of their perpetrator and to stay as far away as possible.

This is how one survivor tried to protect herself from an older abusive brother:

I became a very withdrawn child. I would retreat to my room and read. If my brother was involved in a game, I wouldn't play. If he was in a particular room, I would go to a different one.

A woman with a brother four years older experienced abuse on a daily basis. She wrote:

My brother would hit me, bite me, wrestle me, and so on, anytime my parents were out of sight. The times that were most frightening for me were after school or the period between the time we arrived home from school and when my parents would come home from work, about two or three hours. I would run to my room and lock the door or go to a friend's house so he wouldn't terrorize me.

Abusing a younger sibling in turn. Some victims responded to their abuse by inflicting the same treatment on another sibling. This behavior can be understood in two ways. First, the victim used the older child's behavior as a model and in turn became a perpetrator. Social learning theory states that violence or abuse is often a *learned behavior.* The behavior may be learned from parents, if they are abusive to each other, from caretakers, from an older sibling who is abusive, from peers, or from television movies, and videos (see chapter 3). A continuing pattern is established and, unless the parents intervene, abuse can become a normal way to interact.

Second, the behavior may be understood as a psychological defense. The victim becomes the *aggressor* by shifting from a passive victim role to an active, aggressive role. The end result is that the siblings are in a state of constant conflict.

The worst fights started around the time I was in third grade. I got a lot of abuse from my older brother. Then I would turn around and abuse my sister. I would get her twice as hard as what I received. As we got older, it got worse. I would have knives pulled on me. Then I would turn around and use a stick or broom handle on one of the others. I would take my anger out on my sister or younger brother.

Sibling abuse perpetrators are not born; they are cultivated.[1] Researchers indicate that there are two primary ways that children can become aggressive: 1) by observing others—parents, other adults, peers, siblings, and actors in movies, videos, and television—who are acting aggressively; and, 2) by being treated aggressively.[2] The National Family Violence Studies (in chapter 1) bore this out: rates of sibling violence were higher in families where abuse was occurring between the parents and where parents were treating children aggressively by using corporal punishment—spanking. By their behaviors the parents were *cultivating* aggression in the children. And, the children's aggression was then played out in their relationships with siblings. As the cycle of violence moves along, we might expect this aggressive behavior to extend to peers and to dating relationships.

I recall life in our home as I was growing up as hell—a constant turmoil. My parents were fighting with each other; I and my brothers and sisters were at each other constantly. After several years of therapy, I now call these behaviors what they were—physical and emotional abuse. I think the constant arguments my older brother was having with his fiancé fit into this pattern.

Telling their parents. Many victims of sibling physical and emotional abuse tell their parents, but the parents refuse to help. Indeed, survivors claimed that after reporting physical abuse, for example, they were further victimized by being blamed. "You must have done something to deserve it," a parent might accuse. Obviously, such a response provides no protection from future assaults and discourages the child from ever again asking for help.

Another common parental reaction was to become very angry and discipline both the perpetrator and the victim. In some instances, the perpetrator would be severely whipped or beaten with a belt until the victim felt badly for having reported the abuse. These responses also led victims to conclude that it did not pay to talk to their parents.

Undoubtedly, many children do report the abuse, and the parents effectively intervene. Parents can examine the situation with each child, determine what provoked the incident, identify the contribution of each child to what has escalated to abusive behavior, and help the siblings consider how the altercation could have been avoided. This is the problem-solving approach which is discussed later, a helpful way for parents to intervene.

Fighting back. Although some survivors of physical abuse fought back and in turn were aggressive to their perpetrator, many who were abused (for example, by an older brother or sister) were not able to do so. They were smaller in size and did not have the strength to fight back. Also, some were aware that if they did, the perpetrators would be more abusive in return.

Sibling survivors of emotional abuse, however, often did fight back and in turn emotionally abused the perpetrator by name-calling, ridicule, and degrading comments. A survivor wrote that an older sister would "yell swear words and names" at her. At the age of eight or nine, she was shocked by her sister's language, but she soon "gave as good as I got, swear-word-wise." Another respondent reported, "I retaliated with equally mean words."

A woman wrote about how she handled her sister's emotionally abusive comments:

I would turn the emotional abuse around on my sister. I would make her cry and go into hysterics. She would just go crazy. The more I got from my older brother, the more and more I would give my sister.

Notice in this survivor's comments how abuse was being cultivated in this family—an older brother was abusing his younger sister who in turn was abusing her younger sister. One wonders, based on what we know from research about sibling abuse, if the parents were abusing each other and the brother was learning to be abusive from them. This survivor's comment may also explain why many parents view emotional abuse among their children as "normal sibling rivalry." In some instances, survivors' parents even joined in by calling them names or making just as much fun of them as did their siblings. Emotional abuse in these families became a normal way of interaction—normal, yet pathological in its destructiveness to everyone involved.

Internalizing the abusive message. A response unique to victims of emotional abuse was to accept the perpetrator's abusive message—name-calling, ridicule, and degrading messages—as if what was being said were true. But, accepting the message as reality only confirmed the respondents in their role as victims. The perpetrator's abuse was now a self-fulfilling prophecy that in some instances would haunt them into adulthood.

One survivor reported, "I believed everything my sister ever told me. I was dumb, homely, stupid, fat. No one would ever love me." At age forty one, as a reasonably bright adult, this woman still believes most of her abusive sister's comments. She feels that she is only as good as what she does and constantly tries to prove her worth.

Coping with Sexual Abuse

In cases of sexual abuse, none of the survivors reported that they fought back. They neither fought back verbally as did victims of emotional abuse nor were they necessarily able to retaliate because of limitations in size and strength. Remember that sibling sexual abuse generally occurs in the context of a threat—an older sibling threatening harm if a younger sibling does not comply with his sexual demands. Many sibling sexual abuse victims could not fight back for fear of the consequences from their perpetrators. Perhaps siblings who say no are among those spared from sexual abuse and, therefore, were not in this research. An assertive verbal response, to be discussed later, can be an effective way for a child to prevent being sexually abused.

Pretending to be asleep. A common response of female victims of sibling sexual assault was to feign sleep. Research indicates this was also true of children sexually assaulted by adult males within their household. These victims "played possum" as a way of coping, lacking the ability to use force to ward off their assailant. This behavior also may be a psychological defense against the emotional pain and suffering accompanying the abuse. It is as if the victim is saying, "If I am asleep, I won't be aware of what is happening. It won't hurt as much physically and emotionally." This response, however, often works against victims who later attempt to prosecute their perpetrator. In these situations, unfortunately, children are frequently attacked by attorneys and discredited by juries because they made no protest or outcry during their abuse. Such accusations only add to their guilt and self-blame. Thus, the entire sexual assault, the traumatic incident as well as the investigation that follows, can be psychologically devastating for a child victim.

Acquiescing or submitting. This typical response must be seen within the context of sexual abuse. First, the victims, especially young siblings, usually were not aware of what they were doing when an older sibling engaged them in sexual play. Only after the event, sometimes many years later when they began to experience shame and guilt, did they feel like a victim. They frequently blamed themselves for participating in the behavior, but in reality they may have had no other option, considering their lack of information about or empowerment over sexual assault.

Second, in face of a perpetrator's threats not to tell parents, victims were left feeling partly responsible for the sexual activity. In effect, they were set up to pretend as if nothing had happened lest they experience retaliation from the perpetrator and from the parents for reporting the incident. One survivor wrote:

Once, my mother was suspicious about my being sexually abused by my brother. She confronted my brother and he denied it. She told him she would ask me. Then she waited several days. During that time, he told me I'd better not tell her or he'd get me into trouble.

Withdrawing. Victims of sexual abuse, pressured to remain silent, bear the emotional trauma of shame and guilt. The only visible sign of this on the part of the victim may be a tendency to withdraw, to want to be alone. Parents, teachers, and other adults who are in contact with children need to be aware of this reaction when something is bothering a child. This important clue may lead to repressed emotions surrounding a painful experience, such as sexual abuse from a sibling.

The repression of the experience and its accompanying feelings may carry over even into adulthood. This reaction may be so strong that the survivor is in denial that the abuse even occurred. However, something later in life may prompt its recall into consciousness as the following survivor describes:

I had no recollection of the sexual abuse from my brother until I was pregnant with my daughter. I then started having very graphic nightmares about my brother raping me. I was about three or four years old in the dreams. He was on top of me, holding me down and forcing himself into me. I was crying and screaming at him to stop. He would say, "You know you like it." I thought I was a pervert to have those dreams, so I didn't tell anyone about them until my daughter was about a year old. I was having some problems with her, so I went to see a counselor. In the course of our discussions, I told the counselor about the nightmares. She asked if I had ever been sexually abused. I said I hadn't. However, she commented that it may have happened. With her support and encouragement, I asked my sisters first. They said that our brother had abused them also, but there was no penetration. Then I confronted him. I told him what exactly was in the dreams, down to the last detail. There was a silence; then he said, "You are right, I did that."

Something to Think About

How do the siblings in your family typically react after they have been involved in a conflict with each other?

Have you observed a *pattern* of behavior in the way the siblings interact with each other, for example, one sibling repeatedly avoiding or being fearful of another?

1 Fried, S., & Fried, P. (1996). *Bullies & victims*. New York: M. Evans.

2 Eron, L., & Huesmann, L. (1985). The role of television in the development of pro-social and antisocial behavior. In D. Olweus, M. Radke-Yarrow, & J. Block (Eds.), *Development of antisocial and pro-social behavior* pp. 285-314). Orlando, FL: Academic Press.

My parents acted as if everything was wonderful in our family. Little did they know that my brother was fondling me.

A sibling abuse survivor

Chapter 8

Why Aren't Parents More Aware?

We have seen that survivors of sibling abuse can suffer terribly at the hands of a brother or sister. Weren't the parents aware of what was going on? Where were they during all of this? Sibling abuse survivors report that their parents were quite aware of the physical and emotional abuse of siblings but not the sexual abuse. In a later chapter, you will find out why they did nothing about what they did know.

Sibling sexual abuse was a mystery to parents partly because it occurred only when the parents were away from home or during the night when they were asleep. Also, the victims were unable to inform their parents about what was happening. One would think that children could surely tell their parents, but they couldn't for several reasons. In this chapter, the reasons why children couldn't talk about their sexual abuse are identified. The mistakes parents make when they become aware of abuse are also discussed.

The Victims—Unaware

At the time that sexual abuse is occurring, victims often do not perceive it as abuse. Perhaps the child is not cognitively or emotionally mature enough to understand what is really happening. This is especially true of young children.

For example, a survivor, who was seven years old at the time of her first sexual incident with her brother, went into the woods with him while their mother was working. He fondled her breasts and genitals and made her do the same to him. Afterward, he threatened to kill her if she told anyone. The survivor, now as an adult, recalled her reaction: "I didn't even realize what he was doing. To me it was like brushing my hair." As an adult, however, her reaction is very different. She is aware that this was an abusive incident, the first of many. Looking back on these experiences, she is very angry that as a small child her brother abused her. As a result, she experiences feelings of low self-esteem.

A Sibling Abuses Authority

Children frequently do not tell parents about sibling abuse when they are abused in the context of perceived authority. The perpetrator may be an older brother acting as a baby-sitter for a younger sister. As parents, we often instruct young children in this and similar situations—"Obey your brother, do what he tells you." This advice is given from a well-meaning perspective, without awareness of how an older sibling who is about to phys-ically, emotionally, or sexually abuse a younger sibling will pervert it. In fact, the younger child in this situation might never mention the incident. Sibling abuse survivors wrote:

I remember a vague feeling that my brother was more important then me and I should keep quiet and do what he wanted.

* * *

I was taught to do as people told me.

The Victim Fears Sibling Retaliation

Children may not tell their parents when they are threatened with retaliation, like the survivor who was abused in the woods by her brother. Many young children are fearful that if parents find out, the sibling perpetrator might act on the threat. Moreover, if the abuse is reported, the sibling might punish the victim at a later time if again left alone.

A survivor recalled how his older brother had threatened him:

He would lay me down, put his big fist by my face, and he would say, "If you scream, this is what you'll get." Then he would masturbate me.

And one woman had a similar experience:

I would be in my bed asleep. He would jump in the bed with me. I would try to push him out. I was just not strong enough and he would always keep a baseball bat or knife with him.

The Victim Feels Self-Blame

Victims who do not tell their parents about sexual abuse many times blame themselves for what happened. Because they derived sexual pleasure from the experience, often of an autonomic nature, survivors feel like they have contributed to the abuse. They also may be afraid to tell anyone lest their abusive sibling, in self-defense, report this taboo participation.

Adult sibling abuse survivors reported experiences like this. Moreover, to keep the victim from telling the parents perpetrators often accused their sibling of not resisting. "You could have stopped it [sexual abuse] if you wanted to," they in defense would say, attempting to shift the blame from themselves to the victim. Generally, the survivors were unempowered, not having been informed about "good touches" and "secret touches" so as to effectively resist sexual advances.

The Victim Cannot Easily Approach Parents

The climate in many homes makes it impossible for victims to report their abuse. One survivor did the best she could to communicate with her parents:

I remember every time my parents went out, I'd sit in their room while they got ready and I'd ask them, "Do you really have to go out tonight? Can't you stay home?" That's as close as I could get to telling them or asking for their protection.

Another victim also felt that she could not approach her parents:

Somehow, they should have provided a family atmosphere in which their children—me at this point—could have approached them with the situation without being fearful of getting into trouble.

What Mistakes Do Parents Make?

What happens when parents become aware of the abuse occurring in their homes between siblings? Although the parental responses identified in the following paragraphs are typical, they are *never* recommended as a solution to sibling abuse.

Ignoring or Minimizing the Abuse

A typical response to sibling physical and emotional abuse is to ignore or minimize it. Parents often excuse this behavior as merely sibling rivalry. "Boys will be boys; children will be children," victims are told. Even though certain behaviors are considered appropriate for children because of their level of maturity, the abuse of one sibling by another is never acceptable. **Nothing excuses or justifies the abuse of one person by another.** Several survivors commented on this parental response:

They ignored or minimized the abuse. They told me, "Boys were boys and needed to clear their system."

* * *

I told them once and they didn't believe me, and they left me alone with him again. Then I really suffered for telling on him. I soon learned not to tell.

* * *

My parents saw my brother's physical abuse of me as normal sibling rivalry and did not correct any of what he did. If they were around when it was occurring, they would just say we had to learn to get along better.

Blaming the Victim

Some parents acknowledged the abuse that was occurring, but then blamed the victim. So, the child became a victim a second time, known as *revictimization*. The unfortunate outcome of this response is that perpetrators are absolved of responsibility for their actions and are given the implicit message that the behavior was appropriate or that the victim deserved it. The perpetrator, in essence, is given license to continue the behavior. Survivors wrote the following:

My parents would usually break it up when my brother was abusing me, but with me being the oldest, I'd always get accused of causing the problem and be told that I should set a better example and I wouldn't get hurt.

* * *

I was hurt by the abuse I received from a younger sister, but my sister was not blamed; or it was turned around that I had done something to cause it. She was never wrong.

* * *

My parents didn't know [about the abuse], but they would

84

have blamed me or at least made excuses for my brother. My mother would say, "Men are hunters. Don't trust any, not even your own brother." But she meant it in general, not for her son, the "king."

Inappropriately Responding to the Behavior

Parents often respond to abusive behavior so ineffectively that, in some cases, they cause more. For example, when one survivor told her parents about the physical abuse she was receiving from her older brother, her father beat the brother so badly that she resolved never to tell again. For the woman, a two-stage process of self-blame resulted: first because telling had led to her brother's beating and, second, perhaps in some way she may have caused him to treat her this way.

Another survivor described a similar situation:

My older brothers received a severe beating when I told my parents how they were abusing me. The severity of the beating, however, discouraged me from ever reporting again what happened because I wanted to avoid a more violent outcome.

Or, the parents might inappropriately repay the perpetrator in kind. For example, if a child hits or calls the victim names, the parents would do the same to the child. This approach appears to be based on the myth that giving perpetrators a dose of their own medicine will teach them to stop the behavior. Some parents use this form of behavioral control with small children. They often say, "This will teach you a lesson." They may bite a child who has bitten them or encourage a child who has been slapped to slap back. Even worse, a parent will slap a child just like the child has slapped a sibling or peer—giving the child a dose of the same medicine, so to say. Unfortunately, this form of discipline neither teaches new behavioral patterns for the child nor appropriate ways of solving problems. **By mimicking the perpetrator's aversive or abusive behavior, parents reinforce the behavior.** Actually, the perpetrator may become angrier as a result, ventilating anger once again on the victim or on someone else, as occurred for this survivor:

My parents would yell at her and pinch and bite her to "teach" her how it felt so she'd stop doing it. It only made it worse for me, though. They'd clean my wounds and make up an excuse for me to tell my teacher to explain my bandages and markings.

When they told their parents about the abuse, some survivors experienced that all the children were indiscriminately punished, which only further victimized the victim and provided no protection from additional abuse.

Dad would yell at us and threaten us with a belt if we didn't shut up. Anger was not directed at my brother who abused me, but at all the kids. I learned to cry silently because of my dad. The belt was worse than my brother's abuse.

Inconsistently Responding to the Behavior

Victims often did not know how their parents would respond if they reported the abuse that was occurring. Their parents might sometimes respond appropriately, but other times would not. Occasionally, the parents would "fly off the handle" at the victim, which placed the victims in a "catch-22" situation. It was natural for them, if they needed help, to turn to their parents based on appropriate parental responses in the past, but, victims were at the same time fearful that a positive response would not occur. They often took the risk and suffered the consequences. A survivor described his experience:

When I was about thirteen, I was short and thin. My older brother, who was much heavier and taller, took advantage of this and was constantly beating on me. Also, I think he was jealous of how well I was doing in school compared to him. I complained to my Dad once about what my brother had done to me. He spoke to my brother about his behavior, and I

86

thought it would stop. A few weeks later, my brother did it again—pinning me to the floor and this time spraining my arm. When I told my Dad, he snapped at me and told me to solve my own problems. I later realized he was stressed out from work. Yet, I felt from then on I was on my own, that I couldn't count on my Dad to stop the behavior.

Inconsistency in the parental responses may be due to many factors—abuse of drugs and alcohol, mood swings, stress under which the parents are operating, illness, premenstrual syndrome, and difficulties occurring in the spousal relationship. This highlights the importance of parents being aware of their own feelings when they relate to children, lest they set up a situation where children do not know what to expect from the parents or even are treated unfairly and abusively through no fault of their own.

Joining in the Abuse

Perhaps the saddest parental response, especially to emotional abuse such as name-calling and ridicule, is to join the perpetrator in abusing the victim. The effect on the victims was devastating, for the very parents from whom they had sought protection further victimized them. These victims could turn to no one else. The crying and the sadness they felt is understandable:

My mother would pick up on it [the abuse] and also make fun of me.

* * *

When I was six and started school, the girls took me into the bathroom and put me in the toilet to wash me. Then they called me "Stinkweed." I was crushed. When I got home, I talked about it. Even my whole family laughed at me and called me that for several days. It still hurts. It's something I'll never forget. They still remind me of it.

Some parents engage in what might be called a variation of "joining in the abuse." Parents often become frustrated with an aspect of a child's appearance or behavior that they dislike and are frustrated in their ability to get the child to change. For example, a child might be sloppy in appearance or her room is messy. Similarly, parents may be concerned that a child is over-weight or does not stand up straight. Although well intentioned, the parents may nag him constantly. The nagging may even proceed to name-calling—"chubby," "crooked." The parent's action is out of frustration when the child does not change his or her behavior. Seemingly, the parent thinks this "pressure" will motivate a change.

Behavioral change does not occur through making fun of a child. Rather, it only reinforces the behavior or locks the behavior into place and additionally destroys the child's self-esteem. Also, the behavior becomes *emotionally charged*, meaning that various emotions or feelings, such as the child's anger at the parents, can become attached to the behavior making it even more difficult to change. Rather than nagging a child or calling the child names, a parent can engage in problem solving in a rational way, but not necessarily in the heat of the moment when feelings are running high. Parents may sit down with a child and explain their expectations about how the child's room is to be kept and the consequences for not doing so, for example, losing a privilege such as watching television. Or, for children who are overweight, consultation with a pediatrician might first occur, then, a program can be determined along with the pediatrician or a dietician, such as limiting the number of calories to be consumed daily. Rewarding the child weekly for following a diet or exercise regimen by giving special privileges—going to a movie, inviting a friend in overnight—reinforces positive behavior and helps create behavioral change.

Disbelieving the Abuse Was Occurring

Some victims of sibling abuse (especially sexual abuse) report that their parents responded with disbelief—and thus, further victimization. Not only are they victims of their parents' failure to protect them, but they are also at the mercy of the perpetrator's continuing behavior. Two survivors recalled how this response affected them:

When I tried to tell my father about it, he called my mother and brother into the room, told them my accusations, and asked my brother if it was true. Naturally, he said I was lying, and my mother stood there supporting him. Nothing happened, except that I got beaten later by my mother for daring to say anything and for "lying." My brother knew that from then on there was nothing he couldn't do to me. He was immune from punishment. Never again did I say a word because to do so would only have meant more abuse from them both. I concluded it was better to keep my mouth shut.

* * *

When I tried to tell them about the beatings I was taking, they didn't believe me and they would leave me alone with him again. So when it came to the sexual abuse, I didn't think they would believe me.

Indifference

Even though some parents simply do not know what to do, others, in the case of sibling abuse, are indifferent because of their own overwhelming problems, or they may be under so much stress that they do not have the energy to look beyond their own challenges. One survivor explained:

I told my mother about my older brother molesting me about two years after it happened, and she asked me what I expected her to do about it. I never bothered to tell her about other things that happened because obviously she didn't care.

In summary, all of these parental responses did not help the victim. Rather, in most instances, the victim was further victimized—became a victim again because of the inappropriate parental response. In a later chapter, we will look at a more appropriate parental response—problem solving.

Something to Think About

When your children are involved in a conflict with a sibling and one of them tells you about it, how do you react? What do you feel when that happens? What do you generally do?

Review the headings of the various sections of this chapter or create a table with the list all in one place—for easy reference—as you attempt to identify your response to sibling conflicts in your family. Do any of these headings portray your response?

I told a therapist about the abuse I had experienced from my sibling as a child. He passed it off as if it were not important. People must understand that sibling abuse does occur.

A sibling abuse survivor

Chapter 9

Why Does It Happen?

Why would one sibling physically, emotionally, or sexually abuse another? The following reasons are drawn from the survivors' accounts of their abuse. These stories begin to help us understand why it happened. Some of the reasons cited have been alluded to already and some have not. Nevertheless, all these signals are important and indicate that sibling abuse may be occurring. If parents recognize any of these cues, they need to intervene.

More appropriate and more effective responses to sibling abuse are available to parents. Before we look at these, however, it is important to explore what reasons siblings might have for hurting each other.

The Abuse of Power and Control Over Others

All sibling abuse—whether physical, emotional, and sexual—as well as all types of family violence—child, partner, and elder abuse—involves the abuse of power. That is, a more powerful child is able to take advantage of one who is less powerful, often for the purpose of controlling the sibling, as we have seen in sexual abuse. Typically, an older child hurts a younger one or, when incidents are gender-related, brother abuses sister.

The abuse of power and control with siblings is a beginning stage of pathology for a sibling abuse perpetrator. If perpetrators become aware that they can gain whatever they want by exerting power and control over others, they are on a path of destruction. Their ability to empathize; that is, to be aware of and sensitive to the feelings of others, never develops or is gradually eroded. Empathy is an important factor in being able to establish relationships with others, especially relationships of depth.[1] If a relationship is built primarily on power and control, the relationship rests on shifting sand. The individual in control must continue to maintain power in the relationship in order for the relationship to survive. This means there must be an underdog—someone who is willing to be powerless and to be controlled. No one wants to be in that situation for very long. Thus, relationships built on power and control do not last.

As indicated in the opening chapter, the nature of the relationship one sibling has with another is a foreshadowing of his relationships in the future. If sibling relationships are controlling and abusive, future interpersonal relationships may well be tainted by these experiences. On the other hand, if parents intervene when abusive behavior is observed and problem solving occurs to resolve sibling differences, this positive behavior likewise can be expected to carry over to future relationships.

The nature of the sibling relationship affects both the perpetrator's and the victim's futures. Adult survivors of childhood sibling abuse identified as an effect of the abuse their inability to trust others (see chapter 10). Their sibling had taken advantage of them as they were growing up and then, as adults, they were fearful and distrustful of being close to others. They seemed always to be asking the questions: "Can I trust this individual? Will I in some way be hurt by this person? What does this individual want from me?" The survivors reported that because of the abuse they had experienced from a sibling, they have subsequently had difficulty with peers, bosses at work and others in authority, and even with their partners or spouses.

Inappropriate Expectations

Many parents have expectations of their children to carry out responsibilities they are incapable of handling. The most frequently cited reason for sibling abuse was that an older sibling was in charge of a younger child at the time of the abuse. For example, an older brother was baby-sitting younger children when the parents were away from home at night or immediately after school before the parents had returned from work. Several survivors described what happened:

When my parents went out dancing or to my aunt's home on a Saturday night, my two older brothers baby-sat us six children. Not long after they left, my brothers would tell us to go to bed. It was too early, so we didn't want to go to bed. When we resisted, we were hit. I was punched and slapped by my oldest brother. If I defended myself by hitting back, my oldest brother would grab my wrists in the air as he screamed at me that he would hit me more. He would be telling me what to do and to go to bed. I would be crying hard even more and would go to bed.

* * *

My mother would go to bingo leaving my sister three years older in charge with specific chores to be done. She would make us do the work. If it didn't get done when she said, she would hit us with a belt. Leaving my sister in charge gave her every right to do whatever she wanted.

Inappropriate expectations are frequently associated with adult-child physical abuse as well.[2] Parents who abuse their children physically are often those who treat their children as adults. These parents tend to lack an understanding of the developmental stages of children and have unrealistic or premature expectations of their children. They become frustrated when their children are not able to comply with their expectations; this often results in abusive behavior by the parents.

Similarly, in sibling abuse, parents may expect an older sibling to care for younger siblings in their absence. Unfortunately, some siblings put in this position are actually not mature enough to handle such a responsibility. Other siblings may be old enough, but lack the knowledge or skills to serve as a substitute parent.

Modeling the Behavior of Parents and Others

The physically and emotionally abusive behavior many survivors experienced from their sibling was no different from the way their parents treated each other.

How could I expect my brother to treat me differently, other than being physically and emotionally abusive, when this is the kind of behavior we as kids saw our parents continually engage in toward each other?

An estimated 3.3 million children in the United States each year witness an incident of physical violence between their parents.[3] These children not only witness the violence of the parents but often themselves are victims of parental abuse. Even by conservative estimates, child abuse is fifteen times more likely to occur in families where partner abuse is present.[4] Research shows that children raised in homes where the parents are abusive toward each other demonstrate problems in their own psychosocial functioning, including a poor self-concept, anxiety disorders, truancy, and the display of aggressive behaviors.[5] These problems may continue for the children as they grow into adulthood.

Earlier it was stated that **violence is a learned behavior.** Sibling abuse perpetrators are not born; they are cultivated. In some instances, the abusive behavior may have been learned or observed from the way the parents treated each other. A sibling perpetrator may think, "This must be the way siblings should behave toward each other, too." "Monkey see; monkey do," as the saying goes. Or, in more sophisticated language, this is the modeling component of social learning theory.

However, children learn abusive behavior not only from their parents but also from other adults in television programs, movies, and videos and computer games. This places the responsibility on parents to monitor the violence to which a youngster is being exposed and to demonstrate more effective methods of problem solving than the use of aggression.

Parents Overwhelmed by Their Own Problems

In our complex society, parents may be so steeped in their own problems that they are unaware of what is happening between or among siblings. The parents may not have the energy or the ability to handle the situation. For example, they could be coping with alcohol problems, mental illness, financial difficulties, and marital problems, as these comments from research respondents indicate:

My family was very chaotic. My father was an alcoholic. My mother died when I was eleven years old. My father had many lovers and was gone a lot of the time.

* * *

I don't think my mother knew how badly I was being hurt by an older sister, and I was afraid to tell her for fear of retaliation. She was busy trying to survive on practically nothing and deal with her own problems, and probably she had cancer then, even though it wasn't diagnosed for several years. But I think she didn't want to know how bad things were because she felt powerless to change her circumstances.

Some parents may have been physically in the home but

psychologically absent. For instance, research on children sexually abused by an adult reveals that a significant percentage of the fathers in families in which sexual abuse had occurred verbalized a disinterest in parenting, a failure to attach to or bond with their children, and a feeling of being sabotaged by their wives' relationships with the children. The fathers could not empathize with their children's needs and seemed so isolated that they didn't feel they had anything to contribute to the children's well-being. Some indicated that they had no knowledge of children's developmental stages and thus could not relate to the children. Many of the mothers also expressed feelings of being distant from and inaccessible to their children, although not as much as the fathers.[6]

Parents may not be aware of what is happening between or among siblings in today's busy life patterns. When both parents are working, time that in the past was devoted to the children is now consumed with normal household tasks of laundry, shopping, cleaning, and involvement in personal interests such as lodge or church activities, exercise classes, and so forth. Also, many parents bring home work from the office to be done in the evening, making them more susceptible to being psychologically absent and not aware of what is going on with their children. Or, they may just excuse the bickering and fighting as normal sibling rivalry. To be sensitive to what is happening with the children requires parents to be ever on the alert.

Contribution of the Victim

Another causal factor associated with sibling abuse is the victim's own contribution to the abuse, particularly to physical and emotional abuse. This causal factor is known in the literature on child abuse as the interactional theory.

When an adult abuses a child, the adult does not necessarily abuse all the children in a family. Frequently, the abuse is selective and directed at one specific child, because certain physical characteristics or behaviors may make a child more vulnerable to abuse. When particular actions target a child, abuse often becomes cyclical and escalates. This in turn reinforces the child's negative behavior, prompting more abuse.

It is important to note that the interactional theory of child abuse **does not blame the child for the abuse**. Blaming would imply that in some way the child deserves what occurred, and **no one deserves to be abused**. Interactional theory exists only to identify and analyze factors contributing to the abuse for the purpose of treatment and prevention.

When applied to sibling abuse, interactional theory also explains why some children seem more prone to abuse because of physical characteristics. In name-calling and ridicule, as noted in survivors' comments, physical characteristics such as height or weight frequently make them a target. Likewise, the behavior of some children may set up situations in which abuse is more likely to occur. For example, when a younger sibling makes excessive demands on an older child for attention or repeatedly uses another's possessions without permission, incidents of abuse may occur.

Research shows that some children who have poor impulse control and exhibit aggression against their siblings and peers are expressing an underlying rage. Mental health professionals feel this rage may stem from the failure of these children to bond with their family in the critical first two years of life. [7] Likewise, as discussed in the chapter on aggression, there may be a biological basis for such aggressive behavior in the form of a head injury that the child may have sustained or the ingestion of lead-based paints. [8]

Again, this is not to blame the victim for the abuse. Rather, it is to place responsibility on the parents to be aware of such interactions and to effectively intervene. Using the problem-solving approach, discussed later, may help siblings relate more effectively to each other. Also, parents may need to seek professional help for children exhibiting pervasive feelings of rage and anger because they are a danger to others and to themselves.

Ineffective Interventions

Because parents do not intervene and effectively stop sibling abuse does not mean they are not interested or concerned about the abuse; rather, the way they tried to stop it was ineffective. Consequently, the abuse continues and sometimes escalates out of control. Verbal put-downs, name-calling, hitting, and slapping occur to some extent between siblings in all families. This is not abnormal and effective intervention generally stops the behavior and prevents an escalating pattern of abuse. The problem-solving approach conveys the message that certain behaviors should be avoided and will not be tolerated in the family.

Ineffective interventions, by contrast, do not give this message. The children are not instructed on how to avoid the abusive behavior. In fact, perpetrators, angry at the victim for reporting what happened, often escalate the abuse. The victim may not report abuse in the future for fear of retaliation. A survivor wrote:

My older brothers received a severe beating when I told my parents how they were abusing me in their absence. This only made matters worse for me. They called me a "squealer" when my parents weren't around and roughed me up several days later threatening to do me more harm if I ever again said anything to my parents about the way they treated me.

Another survivor describes why she did not tell her parents about her brother's abuse:

There would have been more beatings for everyone all around. Instead of a constant at-random sort of violence, there would have been a concerted and pointed effort to make people even more miserable.

Sibling Abuse Viewed as Normal

Sibling rivalry has been around for as long as there have been brothers and sisters. The literature is filled with examples of brothers and sisters attacking one another. The biblical story of Cain and Abel is just one. The universality of this rivalry suggests to some parents that sibling abuse is normal. **Sibling rivalry is normal; sibling abuse is not**.

Why does rivalry between siblings occur? According to Adele Faber and Elaine Mazlish in *Siblings Without Rivalry: How to Help Your Children Live Together so You Can Live, Too*, the presence of another sibling in the home casts a shadow upon the life of the first child.[9] The second and additional children are seen as threats to his or her well-being. A sibling implies there will be less—less attention from the parents, less time with the parents, less energy for meeting needs and wants. The first child may even think that the parent loves the second child more. Thus, the new sibling implies a threat. Someone has referred to the birth of a second child as a "dethroning" of the firstborn.

Viewing sibling rivalry from this perspective suggests ways parents can intervene to prevent sibling rivalry from becoming sibling abuse. Each child needs to be reassured that he or she is special, important, and loved. Parents can either intensify the competition between siblings or they can reduce it. The hostile feelings between siblings can be driven underground, or they can be expressed safely in the problem-solving approach. Fighting and abuse between siblings can be exacerbated, or cooperation can be encouraged as a realistic alternative. Ineffective parental interventions, such as spanking, only escalate the abuse and place the perpetrator and victim more firmly into adversarial roles.

Abuse as an Inappropriate Expression of Anger

A reason some siblings physically abuse another is to express anger. Two survivors described what happened in their families:

My oldest brother would come in from school agitated and literally start pushing me and my brothers around. If I spoke at all, I was told to shut my mouth. If I cried, he would slap me or shove me down.

* * *

My brothers always seemed mad. It never took very much to make them hurt me. It seemed to start if I made a mistake— that is, if I said something wrong, turned on the TV, or needed something. They would yell and call me names. It usually started with them hitting me with their fists. If time allowed, they used other things, such as sticks and belts.

Victims developed a keen sense of being able to detect the moods of their abusive siblings, especially when they came home from school. They became sensitive to the abusive sibling becoming angry, even when the anger in no way involved them. From past experience, they knew they had to "seek shelter," as if from an impending tornado, because they could easily become the object of that anger.

This way of handling anger is sometimes referred to as "letting off steam." That is, ventilation of anger is seen as a healthy way of dealing with emotion. In attempting to dissipate anger, obviously, the target of ventilation should not be another person, such as a sibling. Those who support the ventilation of anger generally suggest that the target be an inanimate object, such as a punching bag or a golf ball.

But not all research indicates that ventilating anger will dissipate it. In fact, this often has the opposite effect—it exacerbates or inflames the anger. Experiments with children found that those who were encouraged to be aggressive as a way of ventilating their aggressive feelings did not subsequently demonstrate a lower rate or aggressiveness than before.[10] Still other researchers reported that marital couples who ventilated their anger by shouting and yelling at each other felt not less angry after doing so, but more angry.[11]

A cognitive or "thinking approach" to anger is a more appropriate approach, rather than ventilation. In the cognitive approach, individuals work out their differences by thinking and talking about them. The ability to think and to express thoughts and feelings, including feelings of anger, distinguishes human beings from animals. This ability should be used in the resolution of anger. To hit a ball, run, or engage in some other diversionary tactic may temporarily take one away from the source of the anger and prevent further aggression from occurring, however, it likely will not make the anger go away.

A cognitive approach requires individuals to think about how they feel when they are angry, what makes them feel this way, and how this might be prevented when the situation occurs again. This is a more effective way of dealing with anger rather than ventilating anger merely for the sake of getting it out of one's system.[12] The problem-solving approach to conflict resolution socializes even small children to work through their differences rather than merely to ventilate their anger or "blow off steam."

Socialization of Males

The largest percentage of adult survivors of childhood sibling abuse were women who had been physically, emotionally, or sexually abused by a brother. A persistent theme in their accounts was the dominance of a brother over his sister, or his need to prove his masculinity in the way he interacted with his sisters. This in part stems from the way some males are socialized—to dominate or control females.

Historically, women were considered the property of men, which implied that men could treat women as they wished. Biblical literature, taken literally without regard to its historical context, reinforces a superior attitude in males: women are instructed to be subject to their husbands. Male superiority has long been evident in art and literature and continues in the popular media, such as in cartoons and TV programs. The different socialization of boys and girls and the gender-role stereotyping that results can also be seen in gender-related toys, games, and sports. Boys are encouraged to play with "masculine" toys, such as trucks and guns, while girls are encouraged to play with dolls and mimic housekeeping activities. The effects of this can still be seen in today's economic, political, and religious arenas in which men dominate in commerce, in the formulation of public policy, and in the leadership roles of religious organizations. The lower status of women is also seen in the workplace, whereby males and females may do work requiring comparable skills and responsibility under similar working conditions, but women will not necessarily receive equal pay.

The effects of male-superiority attitudes are seen most clearly in partner abuse. Men's violence toward their wives is often prompted by the false assumption that they must control their wives and dominate their activities. A study of partner abuse found that sexual assault by victims' husbands occurred more than twice as often as sexual assault by persons unknown to the victims.[13] The control that brothers exert over sisters may be the first stage of continuing this behavior later in life—in their relationship to female peers, to young women they date, and eventually in their marital relationship.

Something to Think About

Think about the incidents of sibling conflict in your family. Ask yourself, "Why does it happen?" but don't ask yourself this question in terms of what each sibling contributes to the conflict, but rather what is your role as parent in why these conflicts occur?

Does your role have anything to do with the way you have responded in the past to these conflicts? What might you do differently? The headings in this chapter may be helpful to you in completing this task.

1 Goleman, D. (1996). *Emotional intelligence.* New York: Bantam.

2 Bavolek, S. (1984). *Handbook for the Adult Adolescent Parenting Inventory* (AAPI). Park City, UT: Family Development Resources, Inc. Garbarino, J., & Vondra, J. (1987). Psychological maltreatment: Issues and perspectives. In M. Brassard, R. Germain, & S. Hart (Eds.), *The psychological maltreatment of children and youth* (pp. 25-44). Elmsford, NY: Pergamon.

3 Henning, L. Leitenberg, H., Coffey, P., Turner, T., & Bennett, R. (1996). Long-term psychological and social impact of witnessing physical conflict between parents. *Journal of Interpersonal Violence,* 11, 35-51.

4 Stacy, W., & Shupe, A. (1983). *The family secret.* Boston: Beacon.

5 McCloskey, L., Figueredo, A., & Koss, M. (1995). The effects of systemic family violence on children's mental health. *Child Development,* 66, 1239-1261.

6 Smith, H., & Israel, E. (1987). Sibling incest: A study of the dynamics of 25 cases. *Child Abuse & Neglect,* 11, 101-108.

7 Magid, K., & McKelvey, C. (1987). *High risk: Children without a conscience.* New York: Bantam.

8 Warnken, W., Rosenbaum, A., Fletcher, K., Hoge, S., & Adelman, S. (1994). Head-injured males: A population at risk for relationship aggression? *Violence and Victims,* 9, 153-166. Needleman, H. (1996). Bone lead levels and delinquent behavior. *Journal of the American Medical Association,* 275(5), 363-369.

9 Faber, A., & Mazlish, E. (1987). *Siblings without rivalry*. New York: Avon.

10 Feshbach, S. (1964). The function of aggression and the regulation of aggressive drive. *Psychological Review*, 71, 257-272.

11 Strauss, Gelles, & Steinmetz, op. cit.

12 Tavris, C. (1982). *Anger: The misunderstood emotion*. New York: Simon & Shuster.

13 Russell, D. (186). *Secret trauma*. New York: Basic Books.

Not only was my childhood messed up by my brother's abuse, but I am still dealing with it in therapy that is very costly.

A sibling abuse survivor

Chapter 10

What Are the Effects on Survivors?

How does sibling abuse in childhood affect the survivors as adults? "Time heals all wounds" runs an old adage; however, the number of individuals seeking help from mental health professionals and joining support groups for the abused partially (time is most relative here) disapproves this statement. Physical, emotional, or sexual abuse can have long-term devastating effects, whether the perpetrator was an adult or a sibling. The emotional pain of abuse never seems to completely go away, even when the survivor seeks psychotherapy. Although survivors may learn to cope with their pain, the memory of the abuse does not automatically disappear.

I get so angry just thinking about how humiliating, degrading this was. And my brother has been dead for twenty years.

The following paragraphs describe the effects experienced. These are reported here so that as parents you realize the serious consequences sibling abuse can have. If you are observing such abuse occurring in your home, please take it seriously and intervene.

Poor Self-Esteem

Low self-esteem appears to be an almost universal effect of all types of abuse whether by an adult or a sibling. Research on the effects of emotional maltreatment by parents found that their children tended to feel unwanted, inferior, unloved, and inadequate—symptoms that can affect a person's psychological development.[1] Similarly, survivors of sibling abuse were left feeling they were in some way inferior, inadequate, and worthless.

I lack self-esteem and self-confidence. I cling to my husband and am afraid of a lot of things.

* * *

The abuse contributed to my low self-esteem and self-confidence. I still have difficulty accepting credit for successes. I have a continuing sense of being worthless and unlovable, despite evidence to the contrary.

* * *

I feel unwanted, unloved. I feel like no one could love me. I feel no one needs or wants me. I feel like no one cares!

Survivors of sexual abuse report that their feelings of worthlessness are often associated with feelings of guilt and shame, a combination that frequently ends in self-blame for their victimization. This victim attempted to cope with her poor feelings of self-worth:

I felt dirty, so I sought baptism and religious experiences to cleanse me.

Problems in Relationships With the Opposite Sex

An underlying fear and suspicion of men pervade many female survivors. The emotions that women experience after their abuse by a brother in turn are transferred to all men. Their fear of entrapment by men may stem from the restraints placed on them by their brothers during physical abuse, such as pinning them to the floor. It may also arise from the entrapment they felt in their family when they pleaded in vain for protection from the abuse. Instead of protection, many victims were even blamed for what happened.

Sibling abuse survivors who were physically, emotionally, or sexually abused by a brother held attitudes that can be described as distrustful, suspicious, fearful, and even hateful. This disgust and distrust of men significantly affected their ability to relate to and especially to form intimate relationships with men. The abuse that some respondents experienced from a brother while growing up even influenced their decision not to marry. Several survivors described how their childhood abuse has affected their relationships with the opposite sex:

I am uncertain of men's real intentions. I see them as a source of pain.

* * *

I have a lot of fear of men and tend to use my mind and intellect to push men away and intimidate them the same way I was intimidated. I have a lot of difficulties in my relationships with men. I tend to disagree a lot and to be very afraid and contemptuous of a man's need for me.

Difficulty With Interpersonal Relationships

Some survivors have difficulty relating not only to members of the opposite sex but to anyone, regardless of gender. For example, they may find it impossible to hold a job, or in compensating for poor feelings of self-worth try too hard to please others.

Survivors' comments frequently included the words *rage* and *anger* when describing their reactions to childhood abuse by a sibling. This anger seemed to be with them constantly.

Research shows that survivors typically feel the need to suppress any feelings, which creates more symptoms as compared to survivors who appropriately express such feelings.[2] Survivors also mentioned their fears—expressing any anger, a fear of other's anger, and what they described as their own uncontrollable outbursts. Survivors also related their present anger to that felt in three phases of their life: a) the childhood anger they felt but were not able to express because of their parents' inappropriate response to sibling abuse, b) a continual festering throughout adulthood of this anger (the source of which they often did not know until they sought professional help); and, c) the anger toward their sibling perpetrators that they still experience today. Although many adult sibling abuse survivors have sought professional help, their anger remains a factor with which they must continually cope:

I'm afraid that everyone is going to abuse me in some way. I don't trust anyone. I feel in everything people say or do that they want to hurt me. I always want to take the blame for any mistake made, or I feel that everyone is blaming me.

* * *

It has made me very cynical and untrusting of those who attempt to get close quickly. I grew up feeling if your own family doesn't like or want you, who will?

The difficulty some victims experience in their interpersonal relationships may take the form not of overt conflict with other adults but of compensating for their poor feelings of self-worth. These persons seem to be trying too hard to please others, which interferes with their ability to form good interpersonal relationships. A survivor who holds a graduate degree was a target of emotional abuse from an older and a younger brother, partly because of how well she had achieved in school:

Until I went into psychotherapy one year ago, I did everything I could to be approved of by my family—worked all the time, spent money for their needs at special occasions, and so on, just to have them tell me I was okay. They continued to downgrade my profession and my education. I was always trying to be perfect and took all responsibility for my family. Unfortunately, I married someone with two adult children who treated me as my brother did, and I went through the same dance for them, too.

Repeating the Victim Role in Other Relationships

A significant effect of sibling abuse is that the survivors as adults frequently enter into relationships in which they are revictimized. Friends and mates seem to place them in situations where they again experience abuse. A reflection of internalized feelings of low self-esteem and worthlessness, their behavior gives the message that they deserve to be used and abused. Thus, they unconsciously choose to associate with others who abuse them.

Research on adult-child sexual abuse indicates that those survivors are also likely to continue being abused as adults.[3] A similar phenomenon occurs among women who have been battered by their husbands. They frequently leave one abusive relationship and enter into another, thereby continuing their role of victim.[4] The following comments confirm this behavior:

I know that my brother hurt me because he needed something desperately from me that he felt he didn't have himself. He was a very weak individual. I tend to pick men now who are weaker than me and need a lot. Then I push them away. I also pick men who have a covert sadistic streak.

* * *

It took me into my thirties before I began to see a pattern from the abuse I experienced from an older sister. I chose a first husband who abused me. Also, I tend to constantly be doing too much as if to make me feel better.

Continued Self-Blame

Survivors who blame themselves for sexual abuse often continue this pattern into adulthood. Intellectually, they know such thinking is absurd, but emotionally they cannot accept the fact they did not stop it. Perhaps they find themselves repeatedly thinking that they allowed themselves to be sexually abused, even though in reality there probably was little at the time they could have done to prevent it. One woman wrote about her self-blame for the sexual abuse she experienced from an older brother:

I was told by several women and especially by my older sister that it was my fault because of the way I dressed and carried myself. I am very self-conscious now as an adult of how I dress. I do not like or wear short skirts. I prefer turtleneck sweaters and high-necked blouses. I do not accept compliments very well from men, other than my husband.

One respondent at the age of four was paid a quarter by her older brother to perform oral sex. She complied largely out of fear that if she didn't he would hurt her. She commented:

I have punished myself for twenty two years for taking that quarter from him. I don't like myself.

Sexual Dysfunction

Sexual abuse by a sibling particularly affects the sexual functioning of survivors. Two extreme reactions are common: avoidance of all sexual contact and sexual compulsivity. Some women reported in the research that because of sexual abuse by an older brother, they have an aversion to sex, sometimes even in marriage:

I have been deeply affected by the sexual abuse from my brother. Even after years of therapy, it's hard for me to be truly open sexually with a man. I often experience shame and disgust around sex and tend to focus on the man's experience and plea-sure rather than on my own. I have a hard time initiating sex. I often experience myself as a sexual object to be used and contemptuously discarded by men.

Others use sex as a weapon:

I became very sexually active after leaving home at age twenty. I did not want to have meaningful or strong relation-ships with anyone but to have sex with many men and never see them again, so that they might have a feeling of being used and hurt.

Research on adults sexually abused as children supports the comments of victims of sibling sexual abuse. For example, one study found that adults who had been sexually abused as chil-dren had a higher percentage of sexual problems than the control group, who had not been sexually abused.[5] Other studies indicate that an unusually high percentage of male and female prostitutes report having been sexually abused as children.[6]

Eating Disorders, Alcoholism, and Drug Abuse

Numerous studies show a relationship between being sexu-ally abused as a child and later alcohol or drug abuse. For example, in a sample of recovering chemically dependent women, researchers found that 68 percent of them had been recipients of unwanted sexual contacts from family and nonfamily members.[7] The abuse of alcohol, drugs, and food can be understood in relationship to the poor self-esteem survivors experience. Alcohol, drugs, and food are used as ways the survivors attempt to feel better. Unfortunately, the abuse of these substances only increases their problems in day-to-day functioning.

Survivors reported that sibling abuse has sometimes led to eating disorders:

I have an eating disorder in the form of bulimia and am at times anorexic. These problems have to do with the denial of needs and the shame and hate I have regarding taking things into my body.

Other survivors reported problems with alcohol and drugs. One wrote:

I still tend to blunt my feelings or drown them in booze. I am in Alcoholics Anonymous.

Depression

Depression is often described clinically as turning anger in on oneself rather than expressing it on the source. Survivors repeatedly referred to experiencing depression as adults that they directly associate with their childhood abuse from a sibling. Some survivors' depression was so severe that it led to suicide attempts. Research reports high suicide-attempt rates for adult survivors of childhood sexual abuse.[8]

When asked how her sexual abuse by a sibling affects her as an adult, a forty-two-year-old woman responded:

Terribly! I have seriously considered suicide. I experience severe depression requiring medication.

Posttraumatic Stress Disorder

After abuse by a sibling, survivors may experience anxiety attacks and flashbacks, symptoms of posttraumatic stress disorder (PTSD). Typically, anxiety increases when survivors are in situations with someone wanting to be intimate with them or in daily interaction with peers and bosses. The anxiety is reminiscent of encounters with their sibling perpetrators, where they felt they could not escape from the physical or sexual abuses that were about to occur. Adult sibling abuse survivors described flashbacks of their sexual abuse by a brother, occurring during sexual activity years later:

Until recently sexual intercourse was not very enjoyable. Well, I would enjoy it but could never achieve an orgasm. Sometimes sex would become so emotionally upsetting that, in the middle of it, I would remember the past and the moment would be destroyed, and I'd usually cry.

* * *

Sometimes, I will be thinking about what my brother did to me and when my husband approaches me for sex, I will push him away. I find myself daydreaming about the whole nightmare of my sexual abuse. It's like it's still happening and is never going to stop.

Something to Think About

Mentally put yourself back into the role of a child. How do you think you would react to being physically, emotionally or sexually abused by a sibling?

How might your reaction differ if your parents ignored the abuse or blamed you for it? Do you think the abuse would affect your life now as an adult?

1 Garbarino, J., Guttman, E., & Seeley, J. (1986). *The psychologically battered child.* San Francisco, CA: Jossey-Bass.

2 Scott, R., & Day, H. (1996). Association of abuse-related symptoms and style of anger expression for female survivors of childhood incest. *Journal of Interpersonal Violence, ll,* 208-220.

3 McGuire, L., & Wagner, N. (1978). Sexual dysfunction in women who were molested as children: One response pattern and suggestions for treatment. *Journal of Sex and Marital Therapy,* 1, 11-15. Summit, R., & Kryso, J., (1978). Sexual abuse of children: A clinical spectrum. *Clinical Social Work Journal,* I, 62-77.

4 Walker, L., (1984). *The battered woman syndrome.* New York: Springer.

5 Meiselman, K. (1978). *Incest: A psychological study of causes and effects with treatment recommendations.* San Francisco, CA: Jossey-Bass.

6 Silbert, M., & Pines, A. (1983). Early sexual exploitation as an influence in prostitution. *Social Work, 2,* 285-289.

7 Teets, J. (1995). Childhood sexual trauma of chemically dependent women. *Journal of Psychoactive Drugs, 27,* 231-238.

8 Briere, J., Evans, D., Runtz, M., & Wall, T. (1988). Symptomatology in men who were molested as children: A comparison study. *American Journal of Orthopsychiatry, 58,* 457-461.

My sister treated me terribly—hitting and slapping me and constantly calling me names. My parents said that it was just sibling rivalry—that she must be jealous of me. That didn't help me out, however.

A sibling abuse survivor

Chapter 11

Should We Suspect Abuse?

Some siblings hit, slap, and punch each other. At times they may call each other names. The critical question, then, is how can parents distinguish between normal sibling interactions or curiosity and behavior that is abusive? Four criteria help to answer this question.

The criteria presented here should not be applied in an "either/or" or absolute manner. Human behavior is very complex and does not lend itself easily to scrutiny. Many shades of gray are found in sibling interactions as well as in questions about whether a specific behavior is abusive. However, the physical pain and emotional suffering of sibling abuse survivors remind us that it is wise to err in the direction of protecting the victim in cases of uncertainty.

Before trying to distinguish between normal and abusive behavior, the specific behavior must be identified. For example, isolate what is occurring from the emotions surrounding the behavior, such as anger, hurt, or shame. Each of the following sibling interactions illustrates a specific behavior.

Example 1. Two siblings, two and four years old, are constantly fighting over toys. When the four-year-old chooses a toy, the two-year-old wants the same toy. A struggle ensues and one of them, generally the two-year-old, ends up crying.

Example 2. Sue is fourteen years old. She is angry with her parents who have set limits on her dating. She can do no individual dating but go out with boys only in mixed groups. Also, her weekend curfew is 10 P.M. But Mitzi, Sue's seventeen-year-old sister, is allowed to go out alone with a boy to a movie or a school activity. Her weekend curfew is 11 P.M. Sue is very jealous of Mitzi's privileges, and every weekend she reminds her parents how unfair they are. The two girls repeatedly battle over this issue as well. Recently, the parents overheard Sue calling Mitzi "an ugly bitch" after a heated discussion of their different dating privileges.

Example 3. A mother notices that her four-year-old son is fascinated by his new baby sister when she is changing her diaper. He seems very curious about the baby's genital area and is always present when diapers are changed.

What specific behavior is occurring in each of the above examples? In the first example, the behavior is fighting; in the second, name-calling; and, in the third, observation. Although the last example does not state this, the four-year-old probably also is questioning the mother about the differences he notices in genitalia.

Criterion 1: Is the Behavior age-appropriate?

First, distinguish abusive behavior from nonabusive behavior by asking if it is age-appropriate. Consider the first example: Is it appropriate for a two-year-old and a four-year-old to be struggling over toys? Yes, it is. The two-year-old is probably simply mimicking his older sibling and wants to play with whatever toy his older sibling chooses. It is easier to do what "big brother" is doing, and it is possibly more fun, even though "big brother" doesn't feel this way.

Consider the second example. Jealousy and fighting over differences in privileges are quite age-appropriate between adolescents. They are both struggling with their own identities and attempting to try their wings outside the safety of their home. Sue, age fourteen, does not view herself as less mature than Mitzi and sees no reason why she shouldn't have the same privileges. But name-calling is hardly an appropriate way for Sue to handle her anger, although not an uncommon response.

A word of caution at this point: Even though fighting and jealousy between siblings are typical, such behavior should not be ignored. Nonabusive interactions can escalate into abuse if effective parental intervention does not occur. Ignoring the behavior will not make it go away. Moreover, constant fighting between siblings is unpleasant not only for those involved but also for those witnessing the behavior.

The critical question is how to intervene. Various avenues of assistance are available for parents. Parents can apply the problem-solving process, SAFE, that will be discussed in the next chapter. Courses on parenting are provided through community mental health agencies, churches, and other educational resources. Books that focus on sibling relationships are available at bookstores, public libraries and through the Internet. Figure 11:1 identifies a list of helpful parenting books.

Figure 11:1
Helpful Parenting Books

Cappello, Dominnic (2000). *Ten talks parents must have with their children about violence.* New York: Hyperion.

Cooper, Scott (2000). *Sticks and stones: 7 ways your child can deal with teasing, conflict, and other hard times.* New York: Times Books.

Cray, Elizabeth (1993). *Without spanking or spoiling: A practical approach to toddler and preschool guidance.* Seattle: Parenting Press.

Faber, Adele, & Mazlish, Elaine (1980). *How to talk so kids will listen & listen so kids will talk.* New York: Avon.

Faber, Adele, & Mazlish, Elaine (1987). *Siblings without rivalry: How to help your children live together so you can live too.* New York: Avon.

Forehand, Rex, & Long, Nicholas (1996). *Parenting the strong-willed child.* Chicago: Contemporary Books.

Frank, Robert (1999). *The involved father: Family-tested solutions for getting dads to participate more in the daily lives of their children.* New York: St. Martin's.

Nelson, Jane, Lott, Lynn, & Stephen, Glen H. (1999). *Positive discipline A-Z.* Rocklin, CA: Prima.

Sears, William, & Sears, Martha (1995). *The discipline book: Everything you need to know to have a better-behaved child from birth to age ten.* Boston: Little, Brown.

Consider the third example: Observation and questioning on the part of a four-year-old are normal, as is sexual curiosity. A small boy who has never seen a vagina may be expected to ask why his sister is different. If the four-year-old wants to touch his baby sister's vagina, an effective parental response may be to differentiate for the child appropriate and inappropriate touches. This example highlights the importance of giving sexual information that is appropriate for their developmental age.

Age-appropriate behavior can be determined by professionals with a knowledge of child development and by reading books or talking to other parents. The parents of a mentally retarded child, for example, told their friends that their four-year-old would sometimes crawl on the floor and bark like a dog or meow like a cat. The parents saw this as an example of his retardation. The friends, however, pointed out that their own four-year-old child, who was not mentally retarded, frequently did the same thing. As a matter of fact, they said he had once asked if he could try eating out of a bowl on the floor like the family pets. Thus, the first set of parents learned that this was age-appropriate behavior for their four-year-old.

Now, consider the following examples of inappropriate sibling interactions. A ten-year-old brother destroys his three-year-old sister's dolls by pulling out their hair, tearing off a leg or arm, or stabbing them with a knife. An eight-year-old sister composes a song about her younger brother who is overweight. The words make fun of him and call him "Tubby." She sings it whenever she is around him, even in front of his friends. A fourteen-year-old boy fondles the genitals of his three-year-old sister behind a shed in the backyard.

These examples portray three behaviors: the destruction of toys, ridicule through name-calling, and sexual fondling. In light of the age of the participants, especially the perpetrators, these are not age-appropriate behaviors. A ten-year-old boy should have learned to respect the toys of other children and not destroy them. Likewise, an eight-year-old girl may delight in some teasing, but this teasing done before her brother's peers is vicious. And a boy fondling the genitals of his younger sister is not appropriate behavior at any age. By the age of fourteen, a boy should be aware of sexual differences between boys and girls and between "good touches" and "secret touches." Moreover, the fact that the fondling is occurring in a clandestine setting implies that the perpetrator has some awareness that the behavior is inappropriate. Also, the younger child is not mature enough to decide whether she wishes to participate.

Figure 11:2
Is It Sibling Rivalry or Sibling Abuse?

Identify the behavior. Then ask yourself:

1. Is the behavior age-appropriate?

2. How often and how long has the behavior occurred?

3. Is there an aspect of victimization in the behavior?

4. What is the purpose of the behavior?

Criterion 2: How often and how long has the behavior been occurring?

Fighting, name-calling, teasing, and even some sexual exploration occur between siblings at some time or another and may be considered normal sibling rivalry or simple sexual curiosity, but, frequency and duration of these behaviors may turn a nonabusive behavior into an abusive one. When they occur frequently over a long period of time, they become abusive, especially if the perpetrator is admonished to stop but doesn't.

This does not mean that a single occurrence of a potentially abusive behavior between siblings, such as sexual activity, should be minimized. Even a one-time encounter by a sibling can seriously affect the survivor into adulthood. Recall the woman who at age four was paid a quarter by her older brother for performing oral sex and who complied largely out of fear of retaliation: "I have punished myself for twenty-two years for taking that quarter from him. I don't like myself." Thus, frequency and duration should not be used as the *only* criteria in determining whether a behavior is abusive.

How long is too long, and how frequently is too frequently? A definite period of time or number of occurrences would be helpful, but such pat answers are not available. When a child complains on more than one occasion about the behavior of a sibling, the parents should explore the complaint. Likewise, when parents begin to feel uncomfortable about a behavior in which a child is engaging toward a sibling, the time has come to intervene. A critical element in both of these situations is the observation of a *pattern* that is occurring over a period of time. **Ignoring abusive sibling behavior will not make it disappear.**

Criterion 3: Is there an aspect of victimization in the behavior?

A victim is someone who is an unwilling, nonconsenting object of abusive behavior and is hurt or injured by the action or actions of another. Research respondents who were abused by a sibling think of themselves as victims. They vividly recalled what they had experienced from a sibling as children. They were the targets of their sibling's physical assaults, the butt of their ridicule, or the object of their sexual abuse.

An individual in the victim role may be a dupe or may have been placed in a gullible position by the other person. Many of the respondents, especially those sexually abused by a sibling, had been placed in the victim role because of their powerlessness. They were duped or enticed to participate in sexual activity, were threatened, or were taken advantage of because of their ages. These victims often had little choice but to acquiesce to their sibling's sexual demands because they felt there was nothing else they could do or were not mature enough to realize what was happening.

A victim, an unwilling participant, may not even be able to give or withhold consent. The fact that a victim participates in an activity does not mean that the participation is voluntary. A child may be unable to verbally consent to an older sibling's sexual advances because he or she is simply too young. For example, a two-year-old child is not able to protest her older brother's sexual explorations. Likewise, a mentally retarded or emotionally disturbed adolescent who is the continual object of jokes and ridicule by a sibling may not be able to fend off these verbal assaults.

The question of whether an individual is being victimized can often be determined by assessing how the perpetrator gained access to the individual. If access was gained through game playing, trickery, deceit, bribery, or force, the person who is the object of the behavior is a victim. For example, a four-year-old girl is bribed with candy to go to a treehouse that her brother and his friends have built in the backyard. When she gets there, she is asked to remove her panties and expose herself. Or, an older brother constantly acquires money from a younger sibling on the pretense that the coin size determines its value. In both instances, the sibling is a victim and the behavior is abusive.

The emotional reaction of the person being called a name is an important clue as to whether he or she is being put into a victim role. A child called a name by a sibling may experience embarrassment or hurt, yet others who are the targets of the same name-calling may not be so offended. A husband and wife, for example, may call each other names of endearment that, out of context, would be offensive.

Individuals who have been targets of abusive behavior may not realize their victimization until long after the act. A prepubertal young girl, sexually abused by an older sibling, may experience consequences only after experiencing dysfunction in relationships with the opposite sex or having other problems in living.

Survivors commonly blame themselves for their victimization. Many adult sibling abuse survivors not only blamed themselves for what happened but also were blamed by the perpetrator or their parents. A parallel may be drawn to wives abused by their husbands. A wife may excuse and thereby tolerate her husband's abusive behavior by telling herself that she deserved his anger because she did not have dinner ready on time or was insensitive to his wishes. That she is a victim may not become clear until she later joins a group for abused women and realizes that women cannot, need not, please their husbands, that his expectations are unrealistic, and that his actions are abusive. Sibling abuse victims, too, may have difficulty realizing their victimization if their parents blame them and do not protect them.

Criterion 4: What is the purpose of the behavior?

In most instances of emotional abuse by a sibling, the purpose is to belittle the victim with name-calling or ridicule. This is destructive behavior and therefore abusive. If the victim provoked the perpetrator, both individuals are engaging in abusive behavior and are placing themselves in their roles of victim and perpetrator. Obviously, there are more appropriate ways for siblings to settle differences between themselves.

When an older brother sexually abuses a sibling for the purpose of achieving sexual gratification, the purpose of the behavior is not observation but sexual pleasure. Research respondents said that perpetrators received sexual satisfaction, such as through masturbation or by viewing or touching a younger sibling's genitals. In most instances, the individual who was the target of the behavior was victimized and the behavior was age-inappropriate. Such behavior must be regarded as abusive.

Sexual exploration with the intent of sadism or suffering is also abusive behavior. An older sibling may insert objects into the anus or vagina of a younger sibling with the intention of seeing the sibling suffer. The perpetrator may or may not masturbate. But again, the activity sets one sibling up as a victim.

In some incidents of sexual abuse, an additional person besides the sibling perpetrator may be involved. Children may be requested or forced to engage in sexual activity because it gives a third party sexual gratification. An older sibling, for example, may encourage two younger siblings to engage in sexual play while the older sibling watches or even videotapes them. Or, one sibling may encourage another to physically or emotionally abuse a third sibling. In these instances, the behavior is both abusive and exploitive.

A word of caution is in order. Children are frequently not able to conceptualize the purpose of their behavior. When parents ask a young child who has done something with serious consequences, "Why did you do that?" the child often responds, "I don't know." Although partially defensive, the response may also indicate that cognitive limitations prevent the child from identifying why he or she did something. Children may not yet perceive cause and effect; rather, they engage in behavior at an impulsive level with little thought for the consequences. Nor have children had the range of experiences that enable them to anticipate outcomes, especially undesirable ones. In other words, they lack the maturity to look beyond their own behavior.

Supplementary Questions

The following questions may help in distinguishing abusive behavior from normal behavior:

In what context did the behavior occur?

What preceded the behavior?

What was the victim's contribution to what occurred?

Was the perpetrator imitating something he or she had seen?

Was the behavior planned or spontaneous?

Has the behavior ever occurred before?

How did the victim feel about what occurred?

What was the perpetrator's reaction to what occurred?

Has the perpetrator been confronted in the past about this behavior?

Something to Think About

Identify specific behaviors that your children engage in with their siblings that you find irritating.

Ask yourself the four questions identified in this chapter as Criteria 1, 2, 3 and 4. You may find the questions at the end of this chapter also helpful as you think about these behaviors.

Can't parents put a stop to the fighting and degrading comments from a sibling? My parents didn't and life for me as a child was miserable!

A sibling abuse survivor

Chapter 12

How Can Parents Intervene?

You have read what survivors have said about the physical, emotional and sexual abuse they experienced from a brother or sister. You have looked at the ways they tried to cope with the childhood abuse and the effects of the abuse on their lives now as adults. Survivors have also told us about the way their parents ignored the abuse or intervened ineffectively, which made matters only worse. What can parents do when sibling abuse is occurring? What interventions are effective? How can sibling abuse be prevented?

As stated in the previous chapter, parents must first recognize inappropriate sibling behavior for what it is—*abuse*. They must be able to distinguish sibling abuse from sibling rivalry. Based on the criteria presented in the previous chapter, **if the interactions between siblings are bordering on being abusive or are abusive, parents need to intervene**.

"But what can we do?" parents ask. This chapter discusses the following: 1) what to do when sibling abuse is occurring, and 2) how to prevent sibling abuse.

Problem Solving and Sibling Abuse

The acronym SAFE provides a guide for parents and care-takers to effectively intervene in sibling interactions that have the potential of becoming abusive. Each letter represents a step in the problem-solving process.

"S" stands for *stop* **the action and set a climate for problem** solving. When siblings are engaged in hitting, slapping, pushing, name-calling, and other potentially abusive behaviors, it may be necessary for a parent to stop the behavior. Children might be asked to go to their own rooms or do something alone for a period of time. If the behavior reoccurs, parents should mention the need for a family discussion. After dinner or before watching TV in the evening is one time to sit down together to talk about the behavior and consider alternatives.

Figure 12:1

SAFE: The Problem-Solving Process for Sibling Abuse

S = Stop the action; set a climate for problem solving

A = Assess what is happening, both facts and feelings

F = Find out what will work to prevent the behavior from
reoccurring

E = Evaluate the results

"A" stands for *assess* **what is happening.** The first things to assess in the family meeting are the facts and feelings about what happens just prior to the siblings becoming embroiled in conflict. All siblings involved should be included in telling what happened and how they were feeling at the time and after the conflict.

After a highly emotionally charged altercation between siblings, children often project blame or responsibility onto the other sibling when confronted. They may protest, for example,

"Tommy hit me." "Aleysha called me a name." Parents can cut through children's projections of blame by insisting that each child speak only in "I statements" when describing the incident. This means that each statement must begin with the word *I*. Acceptable statements are, for instance, "I hit Tommy back after he hit me." "I teased Aleysha and she called me a name." The use of "I statements" forces children to focus on their own contribution to the altercation rather than projecting all responsibility onto their sibling. This makes sense because a child can take responsibility only for his or her own behavior. The levity that often arises in situations where only "I statements" are used also helps to defuse the tension of the moment.

Aversive interactions between siblings occur at two levels—facts (what is said and what occurs in the open) and feelings (the emotions beneath those facts). Although assessing the facts involved in an altercation is important, the feelings surrounding the event are even more so. Facts and feelings are like an iceberg. A ship's captain recognizes that an iceberg represents greater danger than is immediately apparent, because of what is hidden below the water's surface. Thus, a captain who sights an iceberg in the distance realizes that a portion of the iceberg is actually much closer than it appears.

Figure 12:2

Facts

Feelings

Translating this psychologically, the above-water portion of the iceberg represents the facts/words/actions occurring between siblings in a fracas. The feelings are the dangerous portion below the surface. Feelings experienced by the siblings—

perpetrator and victim—are important in the assessment part of the problem-solving process because **feelings motivate behavior.** What we are feeling often determines what we will do. If we feel angry, we may lash out verbally or even physically at someone. If we feel sad, we may cry.

When assessing feelings, have the children express themselves in terms of the four basic feelings shown in figure 12:3. Just as there are three basic colors—red, blue, yellow—and all other colors represent blends of these three, so some mental health professionals suggest there are four basic feelings or emotions—sad, glad, mad, scared—and all other feelings are blends of these four. An advantage in having children use these four basic feelings is that parents can prescribe what to do when they experience one of these feelings. For example, when feeling mad, it may be helpful temporarily to walk away from the situation.

Figure 12:3

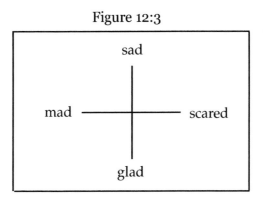

"F" represents *finding out* **what will work.** This is the core of the problem-solving process. The central question to the siblings is: "What can you do to avoid what happened?" Although parents may be tempted to present simple solutions to the problem, they should skillfully involve the children in analyzing the conflicts and how to avoid them. A recent conflict can serve as the basis for this discussion.

The family may wish to set some basic rules that all must follow. Posting these on the refrigerator door may serve as a helpful reminder. For example, a rule might be: No one borrows anything (toys, clothing, other possessions) without expressed permission from the person owning the object. Or, when the door to a bedroom or bathroom is closed, no one enters without permission from the person in the room.

Frequently, conflicts develop around the completion of household chores assigned to siblings, such as taking out the trash, setting the table, and washing the dishes. To help reduce these conflicts, mount a chart on the refrigerator clearly identifying who is responsible for what task on what day, and establish a consequence for not fulfilling these responsibilities (for example no TV for one day).

"E" stands for *evaluating* **whether or not the decisions from the family problem-solving conference are being implemented**. This evaluation can occur a few days or a week later and provides clues for fine-tuning desired outcomes. The problem-solving process is not a one-time event for a family; it may need to be used frequently as siblings and parents confront the complex challenges of living together. In this way, all family members participate and are responsible for their behavior. Patience and consistency are key concepts for assisting the family unit to function with minimal conflict.

On the other hand, every time siblings have a conflict does not mean the family must have a problem-solving conference. As stated earlier, sibling rivalry is normal. Parents can expect siblings to have conflicts and children need to learn to work out these conflicts among themselves. However, when a pattern of behavior is observed over a period of time, it may be time then for a family conference to implement the problem solving process or to review the decisions made in an earlier meeting.

Preventing Sibling Abuse

The following principles, including comments by research respondents, suggest ways to address the tensions, misunderstandings, and conflicts of brothers and sisters. Remember, the more successful the prevention strategy, the less likely the need for interventions.

Building Awareness of the Problem. Sibling abuse is more likely to occur in multiproblem or dysfunctional families, however, no family with more than one child is entirely exempt from this problem. To repeat a critical point: **parents need to be aware that sibling abuse does occur and that not all sibling interactions fall under the category of normal rivalry.** Nearly every survivor mentioned this. Respondents also emphasized that sibling abuse can occur in any family regardless of socioeconomic status, race, or religion. As one survivor commented:

My problems and others' is that we come from religious, "looking-good" families on the outside but where there is a lot of pain and dysfunction on the inside.

Listening to Children and Believing Them. Children may report sexual abuse rather tentatively and over a period of time, but parents should not assume that the report is not true. For example, research on reports of children being sexually abused by adults has found that an overwhelming majority of the reports are true. Actually, very few reports that children make about being sexually abused by an adult are false. For example, a study showed that when the reports of 287 children who alleged they had been sexually abused were reviewed, only twenty eight (less than nine percent) could not be substantiated.[1]

Children telling their parents that they are being or have been sexually abused is a process rather than a one time event.

This means that a child may hint at the abuse that he or she experienced but not come out directly and say so. This may occur on numerous occasions. The reason a child "tests the waters" by hesitantly mentioning the abuse is that there may be self-blame for engaging in the abuse. Remember that perpetrators when confronted by sexual abuse often incorrectly say to the victim, "You could have stopped it if you had wanted," or "You enjoyed it, also."

Sibling abuse survivors frequently lamented their parents' reaction to the abuse, as the following comments reflect:

If only my parents had listened to me. If only they had believed me when I told them what was happening.

* * *

I would tell my mother about the way my brothers were treating me, but she always brushed it off. I really don't think she cared what they did. At least that's the message I got from her. It didn't pay for me to tell her my troubles.

Parents can be alert to children by "listening with the third ear." This occurs through being observant to changes in a child's behavior or emotions. Figure 12:4, though not exhaustive, presents some signs that may signal physical, emotional, or sexual abuse. However, it must also be stated that some of these signs might be symptoms of problems in a child's life other than sibling abuse—the loss of a grandparent, the death of a pet, or the object of bullying at school, for example. Children express worries and fears through their behavior and emotions. The task for parents is to "read" these behavioral and emotional changes. One way to approach this is for a parent to sit down quietly with a child, state that they notice the child has appeared sad, and ask if they would talk about these sad feelings.

Figure 12:4

Signs of Possible Sibling Abuse

or Other Problems a Child Might Be Having

- Feelings of worthlessness; poor self-image and low self-esteem.

- Withdrawal—preferring to be alone rather than with siblings or friends; living in fantasy.

- Bruises or marks on the body that the child excuses or cannot explain.

- A sense of sadness or depression that may be evidenced in low energy level or withdrawal.

- Clinging behavior.

- Fear of being left in the care of a sibling or someone else.

- Sexual self-consciousness; feelings of shame about the body.

- Lack of knowledge of sexual behavior or misinformation.

- Persistent and inappropriate sexual play with peers, toys, or self.

- Shyness, fear, mistrustfulness.

- Overly compliant behavior at home or at school.

- Sudden change in school performance.

- Nightmares or other sleep disturbances.

- Unexplained fears.

- Regressive behaviors such as bed-wetting, soiling.

- Talking about suicide; a suicide attempt.

- Genital or anal injury or bleeding.

- Genital itching or pain.

- Torn or stained clothing.

Providing Good Supervision to Children in the Absence of Parents. Sibling abuse frequently occurs when an older child is babysitting a younger sibling after school before parents arrive home from work or in the evening when the parents are away. One research participant stated:

Parents should wake up and realize that just because a child is the oldest doesn't mean they can take care of the younger children. My folks would always leave us with my older sister. This is when I and my other brothers and sisters suffered. My sister felt she could do anything she wanted to us. She did.

It may be appropriate for an older brother or sister to act as a babysitter when the parents go away for an evening, but the parents must provide an environment in which this sibling can appropriately and effectively act as a substitute parent. Optimally, parents will discuss with all their children the rights and responsibilities of each—for instance the appliances they may use, their bedtime, and whether or not friends are allowed to visit. Equally important, parents should evaluate how effectively the older sibling has handled his or her responsibilities when they were gone. This evaluation should not occur in the presence of all the children because sibling sexual abuse often occurs in the context of a threat. A younger sibling, when asked by her parents how an older brother or sister functioned as a babysitter, may not be able to reveal what happened in front of the older child who served as babysitter for fear of retaliation.

Communities sometimes provide working parents with an after school latchkey program, thereby avoiding placing siblings in charge of each other. These programs, often government subsidized or operated by parent organizations, can be found in a nearby school or neighborhood church. Latchkey programs provide a snack, supervised recreation, and assistance with homework. Often, these programs are free to low-income parents or available on a sliding-scale basis. Parents can find out about them from their local child care resource and referral agency. Some communities offer telephone support services for children who are home alone after school. Staffed by volunteers, the services handle a wide range of children's problems, including those with siblings.

Giving Children Appropriate Sex Instruction. Providing information about sexuality appropriate to a child's age and developmental stage is important in preventing sibling sexual abuse. Imparting this information is not a one-time event but must be repeated at different times in a child's life, appropriate to the age of the child and the age of the siblings with whom the child interacts. Such instruction empowers children to be in control of their sexuality and decreases the chance for sexual victimization.

A positive attitude about sex also implies that individuals have a right to privacy or times and places where they can be alone. Parents, for example, must set rules or expectations about privacy in the use of a bathroom, a setting for sexual abuse mentioned by several research participants.

Parents also need to respond appropriately when sexuality is debased in films, videos, and TV programs; in sexually-slanted innuendoes that one sibling may make toward another; and in sexually oriented jokes. The survivors of sexual abuse indicated that their parents' failure to confront these factors, especially the sexual innuendoes of a sibling, established a climate in the family in which sexual abuse would be tolerated. Parents who allow such unhealthy aspects of sexuality to exist may give the message that the sexual abuse of another sibling will also be tolerated.

Giving Children Permission to Own Their Own Bodies. Children have a right to own their own bodies. They have the right to be hugged, kissed, and touched in appropriate places on their bodies in an appropriate manner by appropriate people. The converse is equally true. Children have the right

135

not to be hugged, kissed, or touched in inappropriate places on their bodies in an inappropriate manner by inappropriate people. Thus, children must be given permission to say no to inappropriate and especially "secret touches." Programs with these goals in mind are being effectively conducted in many schools throughout the country.

Figure 12:5

Red Flag-Green Flag People

Over 20 years ago, the Rape and Abuse Crisis Center of Fargo, North Dakota, developed a coloring book called "Red Flag-Green Flag People." Parents and schools have effectively used this coloring book in helping youngsters distinguish between appropriate and inappropriate touching. For two decades, it has been distributed to nearly every third-grade student in the country. The coloring book and an accompanying instructional program are considered by social workers, law enforcement officers, mental health professionals, and educators to be one of the best child sexual abuse preventive efforts.

Touches are identified as "red flag" and "green flag." A red flag touch is a scary touch and makes a child uncomfortable or confused. A green flag touch is a safe touch and makes a child happy. It is similar to a hug from a parent.

Information on how to purchase a copy of the coloring book can be obtained by calling 1-800-627-3675 or contacting the agency's website: http://www.redflaggreenflag.com.

Efforts to prevent child sexual abuse must begin early in a child's life, as one research study points out. Only twenty-nine percent of 521 parents of children ages six to fourteen in the Boston area had had a discussion with their child specifically related to the topic of sexual abuse. Only twenty-two percent of these discussions made mention of possible abuse by a family member. Most of the parents believed that the optimal age for discussing sexual abuse with a child was around nine.[2] However, for many victims of sibling abuse, the age of nine would have been too late; by this age they had already become victims. Most of their parents just didn't view them as potential targets of sexual abuse—let alone from a sibling.

Parents often fail to educate their children about sexual abuse because they fear it may frighten them. But parents educate their children about many dangers such as animals, automobiles, and appliances without frightening them. Other parents are reluctant to educate their children about sexual abuse for fear they will become distrustful of adults. These arguments are similar to what some parents say about teaching children the facts of life—"they may go out and try it." There simply is no support for this kind of thinking if instruction is given to children at a level they can understand.

Violence-Proofing the Home. Society is very violent, as seen daily on television movies, videos, the Internet, and in newspapers and magazines. Just as a room can be made soundproof or a building waterproof, so can parents strive to violence-proof the home. Obviously, a family cannot keep out every mention of violence; however, parents can develop sensitivity to the violence that enters the home. Violence begets violence and constant exposure is not only desensitizing but may even act as a stimulus for a sibling to engage in violent (abusive) behavior toward another.

An important way that parents can help reduce violence is to be sensitive to how siblings in general treat each other. Verbal put-downs of one child by another (emotional abuse) are often a prelude to physical abuse, and gender-associated put-downs may precede sexual abuse in which a brother inappropriately assumes the right and power to dominate and abuse a sister. Similarly, negative comments about gays and lesbians hardly teach respect for those who in some way may be different.

Nor should pushing, shoving, hitting, or other acts of violence go unnoticed or be tolerated. Children can be given the message, in a nurturing context, that physical abuse is an unacceptable form of behavior. Rather, problem solving is the appropriate way to handle differences and disagreements.

Something to Think About

Have you have observed a pattern of sibling rivalry at home that is in danger of becoming sibling abuse? If so, think about how you might apply the problem-solving method, SAFE, with your children.

Before your family conference for the purpose of engaging in the problem-solving method, practice in your own mind how you would implement the different steps.

Review the six suggestions for preventing sibling abuse in this chapter. Think about how you might implement some of the suggestions in a family conference with your children.

1 Cantrell, H. (1981). Sexual abuse of children in Denver, 1979: Reviewed with implications for pediatric intervention and possible prevention. *Child Abuse & Neglect*, 5, 75-85.

2 Finkelhor, D. (1984). *Child sexual abuse: New theory and research*. New York: Free Press.

I have very unpleasant memories of my childhood. My parents were constantly arguing and fighting. In addition to that, my older brother was physically and emotionally abusive to me.

A sibling abuse survivor

Chapter 13

What Kind of Example Are You Setting?

Recall the findings from the two National Family Violence Surveys reported in the first chapter in answer to the question: Where did the siblings learn to be abusive in their relationship to each other?

Those siblings who are most violent to each other live in homes in which the parents are abusive to each other and in which the children are being disciplined by spanking or corporal punishment. Also, children learn violence from what they watch on TV and videos and from the violent video games that they play.

In the following chapters, these two findings are discussed in terms of their implications for parents. This chapter focuses on the example parents set for their children—the way father and mother relate to each other. The two following chapters discuss corporal punishment or spanking, the risks involved, and alternative approaches to discipline.

Media Violence

First, consider some important questions parents should ask themselves about the issue of violence at home: Are siblings learning violence in the family home from the television programs, movies, and videos they are watching? What kind of video games are they playing? Is there evidence that siblings are modeling violence seen in the media in their relationships with each other?

As you have read, social learning theory indicates that children model the behaviors of others—parents, actors, sport figures, to name just a few. These individuals become even more important role models when they are rewarded for their behavior—violent or nonviolent. The high salaries paid actors who star in violent films, rappers who perform songs degrading women, or sport personalities (coaches and players) who engage in abusive behavior in or outside of their sport give a message to viewers, children in particular, that this is appropriate behavior. Society presents these individuals, together with their violent behavior, as important, powerful and successful.[1]

But more importantly, the questions must be asked of parents, What is your use of and response to media that portrays violence? What kind of videos and movies are you watching? Although it may not be possible to screen out all violence coming into the family home (for example on television), is there ever a discussion or a "debriefing" in your home after viewing such a program? Do you ever sit down with children after watching a program on TV containing violence and ask the children to critique what they have seen? Do you point out to children that the violence portrayed in a specific program is not acceptable behavior? Even though the violence may make for an exciting film, do you mention to children that in real life, problems are not solved through the use of violence?

What Kind of Role Model Are You?

There is no doubt that television and movie actors, peers, neighbors, and others act as role models for children in shaping their behavior; however, the most significant models for children are their parents. Children simply accept in good faith that how they observe their parents behaving is the way to behave. Until they become adults, and even then sometimes not, they seldom question the appropriateness of what parents do or extenuating circumstances that influence their parents' behavior. The latter might include stress factors parents are operating under, such as job demands, responsibility for an elderly ill parent, or facing possible unemployment. These may be stress factors affecting parental behavior, but they are never acceptable excuses for abusive behavior between the parents.

Remember the statistics on partner abuse quoted in Chapter 2. The National Coalition Against Domestic Violence estimates that at least four million incidents of domestic violence are reported against women every year. In the United States, a woman is more likely to be assaulted, injured, raped, or killed by a male partner than by any other type of assailant. Dr. Lenore Walker, a noted psychologist in the field of partner abuse, estimates that fifty percent of all women will be victims of battering at some time in their life.[2] Research indicates that even higher levels of marital violence are found among military men.[3]

The above statistics relate to physical violence occurring between partners. Another form of abuse that occurs between parents is emotional abuse or psychological maltreatment. Unfortunately, because there is no physical evidence from this type of abuse, incidents of emotional abuse are seldom reported to the authorities. Thus, few statistics are available for this type of abuse. However, reports from therapists and others working with marital and cohabiting partners indicate emotional abuse is prevalent. Psychological maltreatment in partner abuse may appear in the form of ridicule and degrading comments (frequently focusing on a woman's sexuality), accusations, infidelity, and ignoring the partner,—all of which result in an erosion of the victim's self-esteem and self-worth. The perpetrator can be male or female.

Figure 13:1

The Impact of Witnessing Parental Abuse

Wanda, the mother of two children ages two and four knew the moment she had to get out of her abusive marriage. Her daughter, Debbie, age four, was continually hitting her. When Wanda asked her why she was doing that, Debbie replied: "I'm just loving you, Mommy." Wanda realized that her daughter could grow up with a confusion of love and violence—something little Debbie had been witnessing between her parents.

Later, as part of the therapy the family received, Debbie expressed herself through pictures that she drew. They were formed of hard, bold strokes from the crayons she used, reflecting dark, ominous colors. Fires and scary faces appeared repeatedly in her drawings, possibly reflecting the tension in the home and the anger she experienced from witnessing her father's physically and verbally abusive behavior. Wanda recalled that she often had to remind Debbie to be gentle with her younger sister when she was trying to show her affection.

There is no doubt that partner abuse has a significant impact on the victim in the form of depression, loss of employment, low self-esteem, and difficulty in other interpersonal relationships. The impact of children witnessing parental abuse can also have serious effects. An estimated 3.3 million children in the United States witness an incident of physical conflict between their parents.[4] The number of children witnessing parental emotional abuse—an even more common phenomenon—must be considerably greater. Research shows that it is very likely that children who are witnessing parental violence may also be experiencing physical and emotional abuse from the parents.[5] Even if the children are not experiencing physical abuse from the parents, the impact of witnessing the parents being abusive has serious consequences for children. Research shows, for example, that these children have behavior problems, high anxiety levels, depressive symptoms, poor self-concepts, truancy, and aggressive behavior. These problems often continue into adulthood, impacting children's ability to lead normal, productive lives.[6]

How Do You Score?

Following are several simple tests you can take to determine how you and your partner relate to each other. Your answers will depict what kind of a role model you serve for your children in terms of the way you negotiate differences and how you engage in or experience emotional and physical abuse. These tests are adapted from the Conflict Tactics Scale, an instrument developed by Dr. Murray Straus and associates at the Family Research Laboratory at the University of New Hampshire. [7]

Negotiation Scale. The first test measures the extent to which you and your partner use negotiation when you have disagreements or differences. Answer the questions in terms of the things typically happening in your relationship.

On a separate sheet of paper, please answer each question using the following scale:

    1 = not at all

    2 = sometimes

    3 = frequently

    4 = very frequently

1. I showed my partner I cared even though we disagreed.

    1 2 3 4

2. My partner showed care even though we disagreed.

1 2 3 4

3. I showed respect for my partner's feelings about an issue.

1 2 3 4

4. My partner showed respect for my feelings about an issue.

1 2 3 4

5. I said I was sure we could work out a problem.

1 2 3 4

6. My partner was sure we could work it out.

1 2 3 4

7. I explained my side of a disagreement to my partner

1 2 3 4

8. My partner explained his or her side of a disagreement to me.

1 2 3 4

9. I suggested a compromise to a disagreement.

1 2 3 4

10. My partner suggested a compromise.

1 2 3 4

11. I agreed to try a solution to a disagreement my partner suggested.

1 2 3 4

12. My partner agreed to try a solution I suggested.

1 2 3 4

In scoring the negotiation scale, two scores can be obtained: 1) a score on how frequently you use negotiation with your partner, and 2) how frequently your partner uses negotiation with you. To obtain the total score on how frequently you show negotiation, add the scores for question 1, 3, 5, 7, 9, 11. To obtain the total score on how frequently your partner uses negotiation with you, add the scores for questions 2, 4, 6, 8, 10, 12.

What does your score mean? First, analyze your response to each question. Then, score all of the questions together as suggested to get two total scores. You can appraise each of your two total scores in the following manner:

If you scored between 6-10, you seldom use or experience negotiation.

If you scored between 11-15, you sometimes use or experience negotiation.

If you scored between 16-20, you frequently use or experience negotiation.

If you scored between 21 to 24, you very frequently use or experience negotiation.

Emotional Abuse Scale. The following items measure the extent to which you experience or engage in emotional abuse with your partner. Respond to each question using the four same responses as you did previously.

1. I shouted or yelled at my partner.

    1 2 3 4

2. My partner did this to me.

    1 2 3 4

3. I stomped out of the room, house, or yard during a disagreement.

    1 2 3 4

4. My partner did this to me.

    1 2 3 4

5. I insulted or swore at my partner.

1 2 3 4

6. My partner did this to me.

1 2 3 4

7. I did something to spite my partner.

1 2 3 4

8. My partner did this to me.

1 2 3 4

9. I called my partner fat or ugly.

1 2 3 4

10. My partner called me fat or ugly.

1 2 3 4

11. I accused my partner of being a lousy lover.

1 2 3 4

12. My partner accused me of this.

1 2 3 4

13. I destroyed something belonging to my partner.

1 2 3 4

14. My partner did this to me.

1 2 3 4

15. I threatened to hit or throw something at my partner.

1 2 3 4

16. My partner did this to me.

1 2 3 4

In scoring the emotional abuse scale, again two scores can be obtained: 1) a score on how frequently you engage in emotional abuse, and 2) how frequently your partner emotionally abuses you. To obtain the scores on how frequently you engage in emotional abuse with your partner, add your scores for the odd numbered questions: 1, 3, 5, 7, 9, 11, 13, 15. To obtain the score on how frequently your partner emotionally abuses you, add the scores for the even numbered questions: 2, 4, 6, 8, 10, 12, 14, 16. You can interpret each of the total scores in the following manner:

If you scored 8–13, you seldom use or experience emotional abuse.

If you scored 14 – 19, you sometimes use or experience emotional abuse.

If you scored 20 – 25, you frequently use or experience emotional abuse.

If you scored 26 – 32, you very frequently use or experience emotional abuse.

Physical Abuse. The following items measure the extent to which you experience or engage in physical abuse with your partner. Respond to each question using the same four responses you used for the previous two scales.

1. I grabbed my partner.

    1   2   3   4

2. My partner did this to me.

    1   2   3   4

3. I pushed or shoved my partner.

    1   2   3   4

4. My partner did this to me.

    1   2   3   4

5. I threw something at my partner that could hurt.

    1   2   3   4

6. My partner did this to me.

    1 2 3 4

7. I slapped my partner.

    1 2 3 4

8. My partner did this to me.

    1 2 3 4

9. I twisted my partner's arm or hair.

    1 2 3 4

10. My partner did this to me.

    1 2 3 4

11. I kicked my partner.

    1 2 3 4

12. My partner did this to me.

    1 2 3 4

13. I punched or hit my partner with something that could hurt.

    1 2 3 4

14. My partner did this to me.

    1 2 3 4

15. I slammed my partner against a wall.

    1 2 3 4

16. My partner did this to me.

    1 2 3 4

17. I choked my partner.

    1 2 3 4

18. My partner did this to me.

    1 2 3 4

19. I burned or scalded my partner on purpose.

    1 2 3 4

20. My partner did this to me.

    1 2 3 4

21. I beat up my partner.

    1 2 3 4

22. My partner did this to me.

    1 2 3 4

23. I used a knife or gun on my partner.

    1 2 3 4

24. My partner did this to me.

    1 2 3 4

Scoring the physical abuse scale will be slightly different from the previous two scales You will end up with four scores: 1) the extent to which you engaged in minor physical abuse with a partner (Questions 1, 3, 5, 7, 9); 2), the extent to which you experienced minor physical abuse from your partner (Questions 2, 4, 6, 8, 10), 3) the extent to which you engaged in severe physical abuse with your partner (Questions 11, 13, 15, 17, 19, 21, 23); and 4) the extent to which you experienced severe physical abuse from a partner (Questions 12, 14, 16, 18, 20, 22, 24).

You can interpret the scores for minor physical abuse (whether you engaged in it or experienced it) in the following way:

If you scored 5 – 8, you seldom use or experience minor physical abuse.

If you scored 9 –12, you sometimes use or experience minor physical abuse.

If you scored 13 –16, you frequently use or experience minor physical abuse.

If you scored 17 – 20, you very frequently use or experience minor physical abuse.

You can interpret your scores for severe physical abuse (whether you engaged in it or experienced it) in the following way:

If you scored 7 – 11, you seldom use or experience severe physical abuse.

If you scored 12 – 16, you sometimes use or experience minor physical abuse.

If you scored 17 – 22, you frequently use or experience severe physical abuse.

If you scored 23 – 28, you very frequently use or experience severe physical abuse.

Something to Think About

What do your scores on these tests say about the example you and your partner are setting for your children?

Is the behavior of you or your partner (positive or negative) reflected in the way the siblings relate to each other—for example, in their attempts to negotiate when a problem arises, in the names they call each other, or in their physical altercations?

1 Paik, H., & Comstock, G. (1994). The effects of television violence on antisocial behavior. A meta-analysis. *Communication Research*, 21, 516-546.

2 Walker, L. (1994). (1994). *Abused women and survivor therapy: A practical guide for the psychotherapist.* Washington, DC: American Psychological Association.

3 Cronin, C. (1995). Adolescents' reports of parental spousal violence in military and civilian families. *Journal of Interpersonal Violence*, 10, 117-122.

4 Henning, K., Leitenberg, H., Coffey, P., Turner, T., & Bennett, R. (1996). Long-term psychological adjustment to witnessing interparental physical conflict during childhood. *Child Abuse & Neglect*, 21, 501-515.

5 Suh, E., & Abel, E. (1990). The impact of spousal violence on the children of the abused. *Journal of Independent Social Work*, 4, 27-34.

6 Maker, A., Kemmelmeier, M., & Peterson, C. (1998). Long-term consequences in women of witnessing physical conflict and experiencing abuse in childhood. *Journal of Interpersonal Violence*, 13, 574-590.

7 This modification of the Conflict Tactics Scales (CTS) is included with the permission of the test authors. The CTS is copyrighted and may not be reproduced in printed, electronic, or other forms without permission of the test authors. The unmodified CTS uses different response categories. For further information, contact Murray A. Straus at murray.straus@unh.edu or Sherry B. Hamby at shamby@cisunis.unh.edu.

Once I told my father about the names my brother was calling me. My dad became angry at all three of us kids for fighting and we each got a terrible whipping. To this day I don't know why he did it, except that he was very angry.

A sibling abuse survivor

Chapter 14

To Spank or Not to Spank?

In this chapter we focus on the National Family Violence Survey finding that answers the question: Where do siblings learn to be aggressive? Chapter 1 showed that the highest rates of sibling abuse were found in those children who were disciplined by corporal punishment or spanking.[1]

Whether or not to use spanking to discipline children is a controversial issue. Some nationally prominent "experts" even advise parents that spanking is an appropriate way to discipline. This chapter looks at the subject of spanking from various perspectives, specifically to help parents see the danger in using this form of punishment.

International and National Perspective

Many countries in the world have banned corporal punishment in schools, dating as far back as 1783.[2] Unfortunately, the United States is not among these nations. Corporal punishment has been outlawed because the people do not view this method of discipline as conducive to the education and training of their children. Seven nations (Norway, Sweden, Denmark, Austria, Finland, Italy, and Cyprus) also do not allow parents to use spanking in their homes. Rates of interpersonal violence in these countries are much lower than in the United States. An evaluation of the effectiveness in the ban on spanking in Sweden, for example, reveals that parents rely on verbal methods of solving behavioral problems with children and children do likewise in dealing with each other.[3] Every industrial country in the world now prohibits corporal punishment in schools except the United States, Canada and one state in Australia. Figure 14:1 shows those countries that have banned corporal punishment in schools and when this occurred.

Figure 14.1	
Year	**Country**
1783	Poland
1820	Netherlands
1845	Luxembourg
1860	Italy
1867	Belgium
1870	Austria
1881	France
1890	Finland
1917	Russia
1723	Turkey
1936	Norway
1949	China
1950	Portugal
1958	Sweden
1967	Denmark
1967	Cyprus
1970	Germany
1970	Switzerland
1982	Ireland
1983	Greece
1986	United Kingdom***
1990	New Zealand
1996	South Africa
1998	England*
1999	Zimbabwe
2000	Zambia

* This ban solidifies a ban imposed in 1986, extending the ban to ALL private schools.

*** Includes England, Scotland, Wales, and Northern Ireland

Source: Center for Effective Discipline, Columbus, Ohio, USA - 1999

In the United States, twenty seven states have now banned corporal punishment in schools. Legislation is under way in more states to enact similar laws. Figure 14:2 shows the status of such legislation across the country.

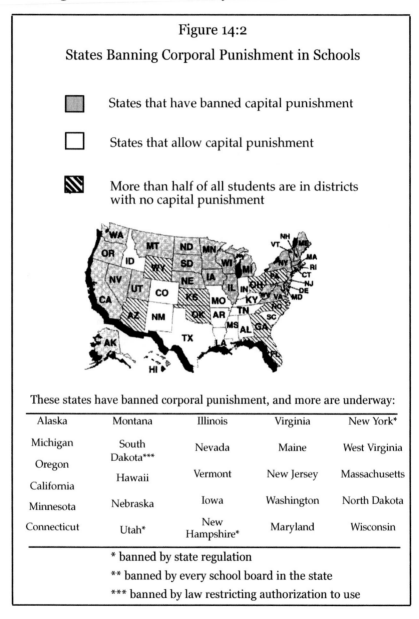

Figure 14:2

States Banning Corporal Punishment in Schools

☐ States that have banned capital punishment

☐ States that allow capital punishment

☒ More than half of all students are in districts with no capital punishment

These states have banned corporal punishment, and more are underway:

Alaska	Montana	Illinois	Virginia	New York*
Michigan	South Dakota***	Nevada	Maine	West Virginia
Oregon	Hawaii	Vermont	New Jersey	Massachusetts
California				
Minnesota	Nebraska	Iowa	Washington	North Dakota
Connecticut	Utah*	New Hampshire*	Maryland	Wisconsin

* banned by state regulation

** banned by every school board in the state

*** banned by law restricting authorization to use

Many prominent national organizations support such legislation, as well. Figure 14:3 shows a partial list of the organizations that favor abolishing corporal punishment. The stand against corporal punishment presents the message that many parents, educators, legislators, and national organizations do not support this type of discipline for healthy emotional development of children.

Figure 14:3

Major Organizations Favoring Abolishing

Corporal Punishment*

American Academy of Pediatrics
American Association for Counseling & Development
American Bar Association
American Humanist Association
American Medical Association
American Psychiatric Association
American Psychological Association
Association of Junior Leagues
Council for Exceptional Children
National Association of Elementary School Principals
National Association for the Advancement of Colored People
National Association of State Boards of Education
National Association of School Psychologists
National Association of Social Workers
National Committee to Prevent Child Abuse
National Education Association
National Mental Health Association

Source for Figures 14:2 and 14:3 — Center for Effective Discipline, Columbus, Ohio, USA—1999

Religious Perspective

A fundamentalist minister is preaching to his congregation and television audience. He shouts that America would be better off if two things were found on the mantel of every home—a Bible and a paddle. He goes on to state that the Bible tells parents they are to use corporal punishment—spanking, whipping—when disciplining their children.

The phrase "spare the rod and spoil the child" often is incorrectly attributed to the Bible, but the statement actually comes from a poem written by Samuel Butler in 1664.[4] Biblical quotations cited as advocating the corporal punishment of children come primarily from the Old Testament Book of Proverbs. King Solomon is credited with writing these passages, which reflect the insights of ancient Israelite teachers about what a wise person would do in a variety of situations. The passages presumably reflect King Solomon's thoughts relative to his views about parenting his son, Rehoboam. (It is interesting to note that when Rehoboam became king after his father's death, he was hated for his cruelty and had to flee to avoid assassination.)

Proverbs 13:24: "He that spareth his rod hateth his son: but he that loveth him chasteneth him betimes."

Proverbs 19:18: "Chasten thy son while there is hope, and let not thy soul spare for his crying."

Proverbs 22:15: "Foolishness is bound in the heart of a child; but the rod of correction shall drive it far from him."

Proverbs 23:14: "Thou shalt beat him with the rod, and shalt deliver his soul from hell."

Proverbs 29:15: "The rod and reproof give wisdom but a child left to himself bringeth his mother to shame."

Several passages from the New Testament also are often cited as justification for physical punishment: Hebrews 12: 6-8

"For whom the Lord loveth he chasteneth, and scourgeth every son whom he receiveth. If ye endure chastening, God dealeth with you as with sons; for what son is he whom the father chasteneth not? But if he be without chastisement, whereof all are partakers, then are ye bastards and not sons."

Those supporting the Biblical justification of corporal punishment do so on the basis of the inerrancy of the Bible and a belief in its literal interpretation. However, most Biblical scholars point out that the Bible must be understood in the light of the social and historical context in which it was written. Advancements in the physical and social sciences, such as references to the four corners of the earth, and possession by devils, make it impossible to interpret these passages literally.

Also, the passage cited above from Hebrews is frequently shortened to the proverbial "Spare the rod and spoil the child." However, Biblical scholars state that this text is very different from the proverb, as reflected in biblical translations other than the King James version. The proverb makes a direct causal link between not using the rod and its effect on the child—namely, spoiling the child. The biblical text, however, refers to the attitudes of the caregiver and makes no reference to the effect of the punishment on the child. Rather, it appeals to providing love and careful discipline, which means to teach or guide a child. Finally, the rod probably refers to a shepherd's staff used to guide the sheep, not to beat them.[5]

Social and Psychological Perspective

There is no research that shows that spanking works better than other forms of discipline. Rather, research points to the contrary. Dr. Murray Straus, a noted sociologist with the Family Violence Research Center at the University of New Hampshire, found in a study of New England College students that the students reported spankings they experienced were less effective than other methods of discipline.

Not only has research shown spanking to be less effective than other methods of discipline, numerous studies reveal the harmful effects such punishment has on later psychosocial functioning. As the National Family Violence Surveys found, the highest rate of sibling violence was strongly associated with child assault, namely, the physical abuse of children that often occurs through the administration of corporal punishment. Other research shows that a relationship exists between having been disciplined by spanking and later engaging in dating violence, spouse abuse, and physical child abuse.[6] In essence, what these studies are saying is that children who have been disciplined by spanking (and may have witnessed parental violence), have been taught that the way problems are solved is through hitting. Furthermore, when these children encounter problems in interpersonal relationships, they turn to what they know or have experienced in solving such problems—hitting. Thus, the cycle of violence is firmly established, beginning with parents and from them as follows:

   to their siblings in physical sibling abuse;

   to their peers in bullying;

   to their dates in dating violence;

   to their mates in partner abuse;

   to their children in corporal punishment and physical abuse.

What Is So Harmful in the Use of Corporal Punishment?

Yes, the cycle of violence stems from the use of corporal punishment. Moreover, specific reasons can be cited why this is a high-risk choice of punishment for children.

Context of anger with possible injury. Corporal punishment typically occurs in the context of anger. A parent is angry at a child for in some way disobeying. If persons are angry, their ability to think rationally gets eroded (see Figure 14:4). When this occurs, the danger is that the parent can easily lose control. This loss of control can result in injury to the child. Most reports of physical child abuse are the result of a parent punishing a child. Review again in Chapter 1 the number of child abuse reports over the past years. The statistics give a picture of how many parents lose control of themselves in the way they treat their children.

Figure 14:4

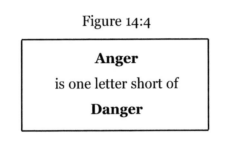

Anger

is one letter short of

Danger

There are two types of aggression: hostile and instrumental.[7] *Hostile aggression* is behavior with the intent to harm or injure another person. For example, a parent inappropriately trying to teach a child not to play with fire may light a match and touch the hot match to the child's hand. The parent intends to hurt the child as part of this inappropriate method of discipline. *Instrumental aggression* involves behavior that may produce injury, but the intent or motivation of the person engaging in the behavior is not to hurt or injure. Instrumental aggression is often detected after parental use of corporal punishment. Although a parent may not intend to injure a child, during the course of a spanking, whipping or beating—done in the context of anger—bruises may appear, an arm may be sprained, a concussion may occur, or similar injuries may result. The first comments parents generally make when authorities confront them about engaging in child abuse because of the marks or injuries found on the child is: "I didn't intend to hurt the child."

It is very likely that was not the parents' intent; however, injury resulted. This is child abuse.

Spanking a child on the thighs or buttocks can injure muscles, the tailbone, sciatic nerve, genitals, or spine. Boxing a child's ears can burst an eardrum. Hitting a child's hands can injure bones, ligaments, joints, and blood vessels. Whipping or spanking a child while a parent holds a child in extension by a hand or an arm, may cause the child to fall and injure himself Shaking a child can cause a concussion, whiplash, serious injury, or even death. A syndrome known as "shaken baby syndrome" is responsible for the death of many infants. A frustrated parent may shake an infant when the child does not respond to the parent's attempts to stop the child's crying. Infants who are shaken are very vulnerable to head injury because of a heavy head and weak neck muscles. The injury often results in death.[9]

New behavior is not learned. When corporal punishment is used to discipline children, they are *punished*; however, there is no *discipline*. Children simply know that they should not do what they did, or they should do something they were expected to do but didn't do. Punishment teaches children to obey by making them feel badly about what they have done. No alternative or new behavior is introduced.

The word *discipline* implies training children in what is expected of them to produce desirable behaviors that ultimately will develop in them a certain character. Even though corporal punishment may have a short-term effect in stopping the behavior, very little is gained either for the parent or for the child. The child may stop misbehaving for the moment, but spanking will need to be repeated whenever the behavior reappears. The danger is that the spankings may need to be more frequent and in greater intensity—creating the risk for parental loss of control that can become abuse. Also, because there is no discipline—learning new behavior—there is no "spill-over" of learning for the child that can be applied to other situations.

For example, six-year-old Danny is expected to put his dirty clothes in the bathroom hamper. With this rule, his parents are hoping to teach him responsibility. Danny's mother notices for several days in a row when she awakens him in the morning that his clothes from the previous day are lying by his bed rather than being in the hamper. She also observes that his room is a mess. Toys are strewn all over the floor and his desk, where he is to do his homework, is messy with papers and books. She ignores the situation because she must get Danny off to school and must leave for work herself. The following Saturday morning, she awakens Danny early so his father can take him to soccer practice. A few moments later, Danny calls downstairs to say he cannot find his soccer jersey. Recalling the state of his room, his mother stomps into his room, observes the mess, finds the jersey under a pile of dirty clothes in his room, and in frustration spanks Danny while saying he is a "slob." Mother's frustration in part stems from the state of her son's room but also from the fact that the room reminds her that she must spend the day cleaning house, a task she dreads. The spanking results in Danny crying and being late for soccer practice, which frustrates his Dad who serves as coach for the team. Needless to say, Danny's performance at the game is less than satisfactory because of his emotional state.

In this incident, Danny was *punished*; he was not *disciplined*. Although his mother "taught him a lesson" for the moment, he really learned nothing about responsibility, the ultimate goal of his parents. Also, he went away from the situation feeling badly about himself, reflected in the way he performed at the soccer game. A child's self-esteem is important for effective daily functioning as well as for his future life. A more effective method of dealing with this situation would have been to use logical consequences when establishing a rule, such as putting one's clothes in a hamper—setting up a chart, identifying the expected behavior and the resultant consequence if not met, and holding a parental discussion with Danny about the expectation to maintain a neat room.

Teaches a child to problem-solve by violence. One way we learn behavior (good or bad) is by modeling what we observe others doing. While this is true for adults, it is even more so for children who are learning and trying out a large repertoire of behaviors. Corporal punishment models that the use of force is appropriate for those in authority to accomplish what they want—"might makes right." And so, when the child is in conflict with a younger sibling, one can expect that force in the form of hitting, pushing, slapping, and verbal threats will be repeated. The behavior may be modeled also in peer relationships, identified as bullying. And why shouldn't the same behavior occur as the youngster begins to date, when, for example, his date doesn't comply with his wishes. The behavior may continue into the marital relationship and into the parent-child relationship, as the child grows into adulthood and becomes a parent.

The previous comments are not idle speculation, nor are they just a dramatic emphasis to get a point across. This is what research refers to as *the cycle of violence*—violence learned from a previous generation and passed down to another generation.

Figure 14:5

There Was an Old Woman

(Original Version)

There was an old woman who lived in a shoe

She had so many children she didn't know what to do.

She gave them some broth without any bread.

She whipped them all soundly and put them to bed.

"My Parents Spanked Me; It Didn't Hurt Me." Whenever the subject of spanking is discussed, invariably someone says, "I

was spanked; it didn't hurt me. A smack on the bottom never did anybody any harm." This comment may very well be true. The spankings that an adult received as a child may not have left any damaging scars of which the individual is aware. But that is not the issue. Rather, spanking represents a high risk to the parent and especially to the child experiencing this form of punishment.

Figure 14:6

Ten Myths About Spanking

Myth 1: Spanking works better. Research shows just the opposite; it is less effective than other methods of correcting and teaching new behavior.

Myth 2: Spanking is needed as a last resort. No research supports this. The example often is used of a small child running into the street. Spanking may relieve a parent's anxiety; however, removing the child from the street, hugging the child, and explaining the danger would be more effective.

Myth 3: Spanking is harmless. Parents use this myth because they may have been spanked and don't want to admit their parents' error in doing so. Hitting a child, even in the context of love, teaches hitting as a way of solving problems.

Myth 4: One or two times won't cause any damage. Although research shows frequent use of spanking presents the greatest risk, yet the infrequent use of spanking does not remove its harmful effects.

Myth 5: Parents can't stop without training. Parents can stop and think of alternative ways to discipline, for example, withholding privileges and the use of logical consequences. Numerous books on parenting are available in bookstores and public libraries and parent education courses are offered in most communities giving information on alternatives to spanking.

Myth 6: If you don't spank, your children will be spoiled or run wild. This will occur only if parents ignore bad behavior by looking the other way or verbally attack the child. However, implementing alternative ways to discipline a child will prevent this from happening.

Myth 7: Parents spank rarely or only for serious problems. Parents often don't realize how often they do spank, including slapping a child's hand. Serious problems, however a parent may define them, can more effectively be handled through alternative ways of disciplining.

Myth 8: By the time a child is a teenager, parents have stopped. By this time children have learned—and probably used in other relationships—hitting as a way of problem solving—something they have learned from being hit. Research shows that parents' use of hitting continues into the teenage years in more severe forms, such as slapping across the face.

Myth 9: If parents don't spank, they will verbally abuse their child. Research shows just the opposite; namely, those who least used spanking also least engaged in verbal abuse. Campaigns against spanking must also include prescriptions against parental use of verbal abuse.

Myth 10: It is unrealistic to expect parents to never spank. This is no more unrealistic than the expectation that spouses do not hit each other. Unfortunately, spanking is a part of American culture. So is smoking. However, the progress that has been made in eliminating smoking in our culture during the past decade can also occur with spanking.

> —Adapted from: Straus, M. (1994). *Beating the devil out of them: Corporal punishment in American families.* New York: Lexington Books, pp. 149-162.

Parents might look at it this way: We are taught as children that the safest way to cross a busy street is at the corner where there may be a stop sign or traffic signal. An alternative is to not observe this rule but instead to cross the street in the middle of the block by dodging between the busy lanes of traffic. A person can successfully cross a street by doing so. However, this is high-risk behavior. Why put yourself at such risk? So it is with spanking. It is a high-risk behavior. Why engage in it when there are better alternatives for handling children's problem behavior? This is the focus of the next chapter.

Things To Think About

Think back on the times you have spanked your child. How were you feeling at the time? Identify the feeling based on Figure 12:3 in an earlier chapter. Again, based on Figure 12:3, how do you suppose your child felt?

Which of the myths in Figure 14:6 do you think influence you in your choice to use spanking?

1 Straus, M., & Gelles, R. (1990). *Physical violence in American families*. New Brunswick, J: Transaction.

2 http://www.stophitting.com/factsaboutcorporalpunishment.htm

3 Haeuser, A. A. (1991). Reaffirming physical punishment in child-rearing as one root of physical abuse. Paper delivered at the Ninth National Conference on Child Abuse and Neglect, Denver, Colorado.

4 http://www.religioustolerance.org/spanking.htm.

5 Carey, T. (1994). Spare the rod and spoil the child: Is this a sensible justification for the use of punishment in child rearing? *Child Abuse & Neglect*, 18, 1005-1010.

6 See, for example, Browne, A., & Finkelhor, D. (1986). Initial and long-term effects: A review of the research. In D. Finkelhor (Ed.), *A sourcebook on child sexual abuse* (pp. 143-179). Beverly Hills, CA: Sage. Maker, A. H., Kemmelmeier, M., & Peterson, C. (1998). Long-term psychological consequences in women of witnessing parental physical conflict and experiencing abuse in childhood. *Journal of Interpersonal Violence*, 13, 574-590. Peled, E., Jaffe, P., & Edleson, J. (Eds.). (1995). *Ending the cycle of violence: Community responses to*

children of battered women. Thousand Oaks, CA: Sage. Straus, M., & Gelles, R. (1990). *Physical violence in American families: Risk factors and adaptations to violence in 8,145 families.* New Brunswick, NJ: Transaction.

7 Buss, A. (1971). Aggression pays. In J. Singer (Ed.), *The control of aggression and violence: Cognitive and physiological factors* (pp. 7-18). New York: Academic Press.

8 http://www.religioustolerance.org/spanking.htm.

9 Showers, J. (1992). "Don't shake the baby": The effectiveness of a prevention program. *Child Abuse & Neglect*, 16, 11-18.

My siblings and I were whipped for everything we did. There was no praise for anything good we did. We spent our childhood walking on eggs so we wouldn't get a beating.

A sibling abuse survivor

Chapter 15

If Not Spanking, What Can Parents Do?

The previous chapter emphasized the risks involved in using spanking and other forms of corporal punishment. If parents shouldn't spank, what can they do? Numerous alternatives are available that are the focus of this chapter, as well as guidelines that parents can follow in the process of disciplining children.

Stop the Behavior; Remain Calm; Think About What Happened

As previously stated, the danger in using corporal punishment is that it usually occurs in the context of anger. The parent is in danger of losing control, if this already is not the case. The child likewise may be out of control. Some rational thinking should be brought into the situation. However, coming on the scene with an extended hand or a paddle and spanking is not a climate of rationality.

A good first step in the face of misbehavior is to stop the action. Analyze as best you can what is happening. If siblings are fighting over something such as a toy, one possible solution is to divert the attention of one or both children. Separating them or involving one of the children in a different form of play may accomplish this.

Example: Libby, age three joins her brother, Nate, age four on the family room floor where he is playing with his toy cars. Libby takes a car that Nate is about to load on his transport truck. In anger, he grabs the truck back and Libby screams while trying to get hold of the truck again. Mother, who is working in the kitchen, hears the ruckus, walks over to the scene, and observes what is happening. She suggests to Libby that she allow Nate to play with his trucks and that Libby do some coloring in the kitchen where she is. Before Libby leaves the scene, mother recalls for Nate that sharing is something he needs to do. She asks Nate to apologize to his sister for yelling at her. He reluctantly does so. Libby goes to her room to get her coloring book and crayons.

Use Diversion

Diverting a child's attention is also a good technique to use even when a child is engaging in behavior that the parent wants stopped.

Example: Mother is about to take Sarah, age two, out for a ride in her stroller on a cold wintry day. Sarah keeps pulling off the stocking cap her mother placed on her head. Rather than slapping Sarah's hand, mother gives Sarah a small toy that she asks her to hold, thereby diverting her attention from pulling off the stocking cap.

Figure 15:1*

There Was an Old Woman

(Revised Version)

There was an old woman
Who lived in a shoe.
She was a kindhearted mom
Who knew exactly what to do.

She raised all her children
With patience and love,
Never once did she give them
A spank, shake or shove.

Her children all learned
To be gentle toward others.
And good parents too
When they became fathers and mothers.

From their days in the shoe
They learned this about living:
Kindness, not force,
Is the gift that keeps giving.

---

*Source: www.nospank.org. 2000.

When analyzing a situation of inappropriate behavior, parents should be aware of the child's needs relative to his or her developmental stage. For example, small children accompanying their mother who is shopping in a department store for clothes for herself or even for the children can be expected to quickly become bored and restless. Likewise, grocery shopping, standing in line at a bank, sitting quietly through a concert, or remaining through adult conversation following dinner with grandparents or guests can be exasperating for a child. The same applies for children's attendance at religious services. Someone once said, "How would you like to sit in church for an hour when all that you can see is the back of the pew in front of you?"

Avoiding some of these situations is one solution to the problem. However, parents who tow along their offspring might at least have available a small toy or pencil and paper for the child. Increasingly, churches and synagogues are providing an exit point in religious services where children adjourn to separate quarters for activities appropriate to their age. Or, small packets of material are available upon entering a church or synagogue containing activities (a coloring book, a simple puzzle, a colorful shoelace to be threaded through a picture) that will involve the child's attention during the religious service.

Parents often forget that children's needs are very different from those of adults. Children are curious, noisy, willful, impatient, demanding, creative, messy, forgetful, fearful, self-centered, and full of energy. Some of the conflicts parents have with their children may stem from the failure to remember that children are children. They are not miniature adults.

Changing the environment is another form of diversion. For example, if a toddler continually gets into the cupboard where mother's pots and pans are located, placing a childlock on the door is an easy solution. A simple latch or hook placed out of reach will keep the child out of bathrooms and other forbidden rooms.

Provide Information to Children

Offer a reason. Rather than angrily saying "no" or "don't' do that," direct your child to what he or she can do. Providing a reason for your action is also appropriate. Although small children may not have the cognitive capacity to solve complex problems, they are able to take in information, process it, retain it, and to some extent recall or apply it in a future context.

Example: Mikey, age four, is playing with a friend he was allowed to invite over for the afternoon. They decide to play with his collection of trucks on the new living room carpet. Rather than yelling at Mikey about not playing on the new carpet with his trucks, some of which had been in the sandbox, mother gently leads Mikey and his friend to the family room and sets up a place there where they can play. She informs him that the living room is primarily a place where adults visit with each other, not a place where children play with toys.

* * *

Example: Mother finds three-year-old Trisha coloring on the wall of her bedroom. Recently, Trisha's father painted the room and mother assumes Trisha, having watched him painting, may be wanting to color on them, too. Mother informs Trisha that coloring on walls is "a no-no." Mother demonstrates with a rag and solvent how difficult it is to remove the crayon marks. She picks up Trisha's crayon box and a coloring book and gives her the choice of two places where she can color—on the desk in her room or at the kitchen table. Trisha decides to color at the kitchen table where she can be close to her mother.

Allow choices. The latter example also demonstrates another technique that you can use in relating to your children and avoiding the use of corporal punishment—giving the child some choices rather than commands. Choice or decision making empowers children, gives them the feeling of having some responsibility over their lives. Commands, on the other hand, invite a power struggle between the parent and child. Along with choices, you may at times wish to consider making some small concessions. This also allows children some feeling of control over their life.

Example: Maria and her parents come home very late one evening after visiting Maria's grandparents in a neighboring city. Maria fell asleep in the car and had to be awakened when arriving at home. Consequently, she was very cranky and uncooperative when it came to getting ready to go to bed. Maria didn't want to do anything—go into the house, put on her pajamas, wash her face, or brush her teeth. In order to avoid a conflict, Maria's mother commented that because Maria was so tired, she would not need to wash her face and brush her teeth that evening.

Negotiate. Negotiating with a child is another way to avoid simply barking out a command that may set up a power struggle with your child. Negotiating builds on allowing a child to make choices.

Example: Four-year-old Brad is having a great time playing on the swing set at the park while his mother sits nearby keeping an eye on him. It comes time to leave when Brad and his mother must go by school to pick up Brad's older sister. Brad does not want to leave the park because he is having so much fun. Rather than barking a command, mother uses negotiation. They agree that he can swing for two minutes more and then they must leave. When the two minutes are up, Brad willingly goes to the car with his mother.

Demonstrate behavior. Providing information also includes demonstrating for the child appropriate behavior. A small boy may be fascinated by his new baby sister when she arrives home from the hospital. However, the parents may need to show the appropriate way "big brother" can touch his sister's cheeks or hold her hand.

Example: Andrew, age three, has discovered the family cat, Scooter. His interactions with the cat recently have consisted of holding onto Scooter's leg or tail while the cat hisses and tries to make a quick exit. Instead, father demonstrates how Andrew can gently stroke their pet and say, "Nice Scooter."

Coaching in advance. Even though you will want to avoid most situations in which your children must sit quietly and behave, there are certain special events you may wish to have the children attend, (for example, a wedding, funeral, graduation exercise, or a holiday dinner where the children will be seated with adults). In these instances, it is helpful to prepare your child in advance. Think about this from the child's perspective. The child may have never attended such an event, which in itself might lead to restless or inappropriate behavior. Or, he or she may just simply not know what is expected. Telling children to be quiet repeatedly through the event, pinching them when they misbehave, or in anger removing them to give them a paddling are inappropriate parental responses. If preparation occurs in advance, children will have some idea regarding how to act. Also, if they misbehave, give a quiet reminder of your earlier discussion.

Be Aware of Feelings—Yours and Your Child's

Figure 12:3 in an earlier chapter identified four basic feel-ings—sad, glad, mad, scared. You can use it to understand the feelings underlying behavioral reactions and conflict situations, as with the example of the ship captain who recognizes the hidden dangers of an iceberg. When working with a sibling conflict, consider both the perpetrator and the victim. Recognizing and allowing each to express feelings is an impor-tant step in the problem-solving process.

Example: Brad, age thirteen, went into his twin sister Harriet's room and borrowed her tennis racket without permission. He failed to return it when he was finished. A few days later, when Harriet wanted to play tennis with a group of friends, she could not find her racket. Later in the day, Harriet found out what had happened to it. She and Brad engaged in some pushing and shoving of each other while at the same time using verbally abusive language. At dinner, the twins' parents explored with each of them what they were feeling at the time. Feelings of anger dominated the discussion on the part of both twins. Harriet was angry that the racket was borrowed without permission; Brad was angry at the response of his sister when he forgot to return the racket. The parents focused in the discussion on helping the teens develop an awareness of the linkage between their feelings and their inappropriate behavior. Alternative ways of handling the situation were also discussed.

Are you aware of your own feelings when observing your siblings fighting with each other or when your child disappoints you by engaging in inappropriate behavior? You can use the same four basic feelings to analyze your emotions—sad, glad, mad, scared. When you are disappointed, it is appropriate to talk about the feeling of sadness you have experienced. Likewise, it is appropriate to talk about "mad" feelings that parents experience when fighting and name-calling occur between siblings. The discussion should include the fact that you as parents do not act out these feelings in terms of hitting and shoving or using verbally abusive names, but rather talk about the behavior and how it can be avoided.

Take a Parental Break

When siblings are fighting and emotions are running high, a parent may stop the action but not become involved in the conflict. Problem solving might best occur later in the day when emotions have returned to normal. Perhaps, the parent needs to leave the room after the siblings have separated and regain composure by taking a walk, drinking a cup of coffee or tea, or meditating.

At times one hears parents of small children saying that they refuse to use a baby-sitter or a day care center for their children. Parents need a break. Meritorious awards are not given to those who continually have their children with them, taking them everywhere they go. Going out for dinner, taking in a movie or play, or spending a night away from home provide parents with valuable periods of respite, an important element in a keeping a healthy marriage.

Use Logical Consequences

What keeps us from not going to work some morning when we don't feel like it? What deters us from speeding down a street? Why do we pay our utility bills? The response to each of these questions is: "logical consequences." If we don't go to work, the logical consequence is that we will lose our job. If we speed, we may get a costly ticket. If we don't pay our utility bills, our power will be turned off. Logical consequences control many aspects of life: "If you do this, this will happen; if you don't do this, this will happen."

Children learn or internalize what is expected of them by experiencing logical consequences. If two siblings playing a game are constantly fighting, a logical consequence may be to stop the game and have each spend time alone in their room. When siblings fight over assigned tasks they are to do, such as setting the table, emptying the dishwasher, or taking out the trash, the logical consequence may be the loss of certain privileges, such as not watching TV or not going to a movie on the weekend.

The use of logical consequences implies that you must be clear regarding what is expected—ways children are to behave toward each other and tasks they are to do. Regarding the latter, remember also to identify the logical consequence for failing to do assigned tasks. You might set up a schedule or chart to be posted inside a cupboard door or on the refrigerator.

Example: Mark, Jane, and Tim, ages fourteen, thirteen, and ten, respectively, continually fight over which household tasks each is to do. They complain about not liking the task they have been assigned and argue about perceived unfairness of time differentials in completing the task. In a family conference, the children and parents discussed how this problem might be handled. The parents were firm in stating that not doing the tasks was not an option. The children, with their parents' approval, agreed on a method of rotating the tasks among the three of them on a weekly basis. A logical consequence for failing to do the task was agreed upon for each job. The children then drew up a chart for the month showing each task, who was responsible, and the logical consequences of not doing the tasks.

A variation of logical consequences is what some parents call "three strikes and you're out." If you are trying to stop sibling abusive behavior, such as name calling or hitting, place three small slips of paper or "tickets" under a magnet on the front of the refrigerator. Inform your children that every time they are observed engaging in the behavior, a ticket will be removed from the refrigerator. When three tickets are removed in any one period of time, such as a day, over several days, or a week, the siblings have "struck out" and must pay the consequence. The consequences, to be identified in advance, may be going to their room for a period of time or losing a privilege.

Treat Each Sibling Uniquely

When parents have more than one child, they often become concerned that each child is treated equally. Basically, this is a good principle to follow relative to material goods. If you were a child, you wouldn't want your parents to lavish gifts on your sibling for his or her birthday and not give you anything on your

176

special day. However, when it comes to emotional needs, children differ greatly. Any parent who has more than one child can attest to differences that are noted between or among siblings. For example, the favorite food of one is the least liked food of another. A sport or game one child enjoys may be of no interest to the other. Differences also exist between or among siblings relative to emotional needs due to differences in temperament. One child may be very easy to get along with and make few emotional demands as compared to the next child who may be difficult to relate to at times and place much greater emotional demand on the parents.

Adele Faber and Elaine Mazlish in their book, *Siblings Without Rivalry: How To Help Your Children Live Together So You Can Live Too,* state that children don't need to be treated equally but rather uniquely. The authors are especially referring to children's emotional needs. Some children may need more attention or more assurance of parental love, and they may be more demanding in getting this.

How does this unique treatment translate into daily living? Parents should first appraise the level of their child's emotional needs in relation to his or her siblings. Next, parents need to ask themselves how to *uniquely* meet the needs of this child. One child may require more hugs—a feeling of closeness to the parent—as compared to a sibling who may be more independent.

Treating each child uniquely also means that parents must be cautious when making comparisons between or among siblings. Perhaps you experienced such a comparison in school when entering the class that your older sibling had attended a few years before. The teacher may have been expecting the same high level of performance from you that your sibling gave. How unfair! Your sibling might be a whiz at Spanish but maybe you are not, or are not really even interested in the subject. Parents also fall into the dangerous game of making such comparisons. Yet, some siblings may not be as neat as others, may not follow rules as carefully, or may experience anger more easily. Parental awareness of these differences and taking them into account when relating to children help them to effectively respond to sibling conflicts.

Reward Positive Sibling Interactions

If you were to analyze all communication with your children, would your conversations be heavily loaded with the word "*don't*?" "Don't be so messy." "Don't track mud into the house." "Don't leave your clothes lying around." "Don't call your sister names." "Don't fight with your brother." Negative behaviors are very obvious and come to your attention immediately. And so you pick up on these behaviors. However, in doing so you may overlook or take for granted your children's positive behaviors with each other.

When siblings are interacting in a positive manner, such as playing nicely together, sharing a possession with the other, verbal note should be made of this. A parent may say, for example, "Mark, I noticed this afternoon how nicely you played with your sister. I'm really proud of you." Positive behaviors that are reinforced by verbal praise from parents give children positive feelings about themselves. This helps children develop good self-esteem. When parents reward positive behaviors, siblings will be more likely to repeat them.

Something To Think About

How often during the past week have you complimented your child for something positive he or she did? Recall a situation where you could have done this. Think about how you might have done so.

Think about the comparisons you make between your children? Identify ways you might relate *uniquely* to each.

Chapter 16

A Final Word

Most of you who are reading this book are doing so because you have some concern with the way your children are treating each other. For others, you may be interested in sibling abuse because of what happened to you earlier in your life; namely, a sibling physically, emotionally, or sexually abused you. This final chapter is for both of you.

If You Are Experiencing Sibling Abuse in Your Family

For many, your interest in this book stems from concern over what is happening between the siblings in your family. For example, you may have observed that an older sibling continually makes fun of his younger sister, or, one child is continually hitting another. As parents, you have talked to them about this behavior, but they persist in their abusive behavior. The problem does not seem to get better.

You have probably been tempted to look the other way and say the situation will resolve itself—"it is a phase they are going through," or "it's normal sibling rivalry." The preceding pages you have read caution you not to take this approach and deep down you know you must find another way. You may have attempted to use the solutions discussed in this book, such as implementing the problem-solving process SAFE or trying some of the alternative ways of disciplining other than the use of spanking. Perhaps even these did not work.

One alternative is to seek professional help. However, maybe you are reluctant to do so. This may seem to you like admitting defeat. When it comes to problems-in-living, however, many parents believe that they should have been endowed from birth with the knowledge of how to be good parents and to tackle any problem that may arise. This is just simply not true.

Think of the following. Your car needs repairs. Why don't you simply lift up the hood or jack up the car and begin work? Obviously, you can't. You don't have the knowledge and skills to do so. You were not born with this ability; you must learn. Why should parenting be any different?

One possible reason some people associate seeking professional help with admitting defeat has to do with being taught some bad psychology—perhaps in a child development class. It used to be thought that environment has the most effect on the physical and emotional development of a child. Educators emphasized the overall importance of the way a parent nurtures a child to the exclusion of what the child contributes in terms of genetic endowment. This is referred to as the *nurture* side of the nature versus nurture controversy. Unfortunately, an overemphasis on nurture resulted in the impression that children are born like a tabula rasa, or clean slate, and that how they turn out is entirely the responsibility or "the fault" of the parents. Obviously, parents are a tremendous influence on children; however, other factors must be considered, a significant one being genetic differences that affect behavior, such as differences in temperament. This is known as *nature*.

When I worked at one time as a therapist in a mental health center, parents often came to me with behavioral problems they were having with a second or third child. Their problems frequently focused on the relationship of one sibling to another. The parents would describe how easy their first child had been to raise from day one. Then came a second child. However, the methods they had used when raising this child when feeding, setting limits, and getting along with siblings did not seem to work

The parents would wring their hands in the consultation room and say, "What did we do wrong?" However, that is not the right question! Rather, it is: "what is so different about this second child, so that what we did with the first one is not working?" Two children from the same family may be very different individuals. Consequently, parents need to treat the second child differently. If what they are doing does not seem to be working, seeking professional help may be the answer.

Where can parents go for help? Agencies and mental health professionals ready to assist parents are listed in the yellow pages of the telephone directory under the heading "Marriage, Family, and Child, and Individual Counselors." Private therapists in practice as well as social agencies offer these services. Social agencies generally do not charge as much for their services as compared to therapists in private practice because the social agencies may be underwritten in part by tax funds or subsidized by United Way contributions. A family wishing to use a therapist in private practice, however, should inquire if the fee is covered by their health insurance.

The ad in the phone book or a telephone call can provide information about the credentials of a private therapist. If licensing of counselors is required in the state where you live, ask if the therapist is licensed. Also inquire if the therapist is a member of a professional association, such as the American Association of Marriage and Family Therapists (AAMFT), the American Psychological Association (APA), or the National Association of Social Workers (NASW).

A word of caution: A family should not seek professional help with the attitude that the child is going to be "fixed." Although the child is the focus of the attention, he or she is simply the one who is expressing the stress that other family members may also be experiencing, including the fact that the parents may be abusing each other. A family seeking professional help for one member can expect the entire family to be involved in family therapy. Involving everyone helps the counselor understand what is really happening so that the family can begin to make some changes. A family is a social system, just like the human body is a physical system. If one part of the body is not working correctly, other parts are affected. If one family member is experiencing problems and taking it out on another, such as through physical or emotional sibling abuse, the entire family feels it. Thus, in families where sibling abuse is a problem, treatment will most likely involve the family as a unit rather than just the perpetrators and victim.

Seeking professional help is a sign of strength, not weakness. By seeking professional help, parents are telling their children that they love them. It's like saying, "We know you are not happy. We are concerned. We love you, and we want to do something about this. Let's get some help for our family."

If You Were Abused by a Sibling

Some of you may have experienced abuse from a sibling. Over the years, you may have denied what happened to you, blamed yourself in part for what occurred, or tried to pass it off as a bad case of sibling rivalry. You may be wrestling with some of the effects of this abuse now—problems with drugs and alcohol, depression, low self-esteem, difficulty with interpersonal relationships, and other problems. Perhaps it is time that you recognize what happened to you was not your fault, but that it was abuse—physical, emotional, or sexual abuse by a sibling.

Often when I speak before groups on this subject, someone lingers behind to tell me about some childhood abuse from a sibling. In the course of the conversation, the person will inquire: "I want my sibling to apologize for the abuse, but he or she won't. Am I wrong to insist on this? How can I get an apology?" My response to these questions is that it is not wrong to want a sibling to apologize. Whenever we are hurt by someone, it is only natural to expect amends. But remember, it is also natural for individuals who have done wrong to be defensive—to project the blame elsewhere, especially on the victim. Thus, to attempt to extract a confession from your perpetrator, a confession with which you will be satisfied, is probably futile.

Save that energy you are investing on trying to get an apology. Take that energy and apply it to yourself. Get healing for the wounds you are experiencing in your life now as an adult. Follow the suggestions in the paragraphs above on how to go about getting professional help. You cannot take responsibility for your perpetrator's life, but you can for your own life. Seeking professional help is one way of doing that. You will find the healing you will experience will be well worth the effort.

Vernon R. Wiehe, Ph.D.

Index

About the Author

Dr. Vernon R. Wiehe

Vernon R. Wiehe, Ph.D. is a professor in the College of Social Work at the University of Kentucky. He holds a masters of divinity degree from Concordia Seminary, St. Louis and a master of arts degree from the University of Chicago. He did postgraduate work in the Program of Advanced Studies in Social Work at Smith College, Northhampton, Massachusetts. He received his doctorate from the George Warren Brown School of Social Work at Washington University, St. Louis.

Dr. Wiehe is the author of over fifty articles in social science journals as well as the following books: *Working with Child Abuse & Neglect; Sibling Abuse: Hidden Physical, Emotional and Sexual Trauma; Perilous Rivalry: When Siblings Become Abusive; Brother/Sister Hurt; Intimate Betrayal: Understanding and Responding to the Trauma of Acquaintance Rape; Understanding Family Violence.*

Dr. Wiehe has lectured extensively on the subject of family violence to lay and professional audiences in the United States and abroad. Dr. Wiehe has appeared on numerous television and radio talk shows discussing family violence, including *Phil Donahue* and *Sonya Live*.

CEDAR FORT, INCORPORATED
Order Form

Name:_____

Address: _____

City: _____ State: _____ Zip: _____

Phone: (   ) _____ Daytime phone: (   ) _____

What Parents Need to Know About Sibling Abuse

Quantity: _____ @ $12.95 each: _____

plus $3.49 shipping & handling for the first book: _____

(add 99¢ shipping for each additional book)

Utah residents add 6.25% for state sales tax: _____

TOTAL: _____

Mail this form and payment to:

Cedar Fort, Inc.

925 North Main St.

Springville, UT 84663

You can also order on our website **www.cedarfort.com**

or e-mail us at sales@cedarfort.com or call 1-800-SKYBOOK

9 26575 75864 4